The Greatest Email Marketing & SEO Tactics

★ ★ ★ ★ ★

To Scale Your Business!

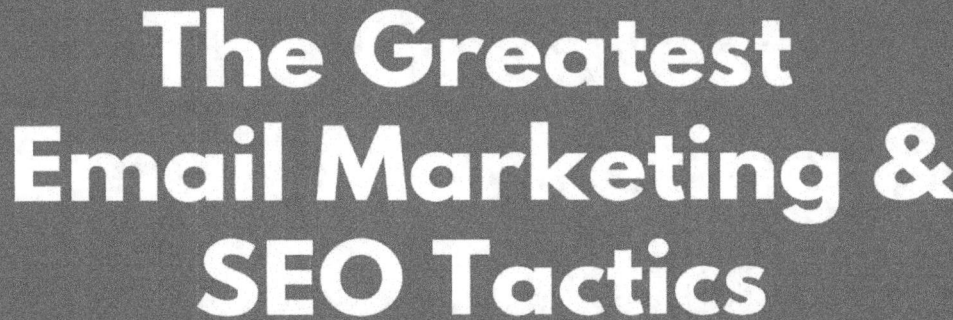

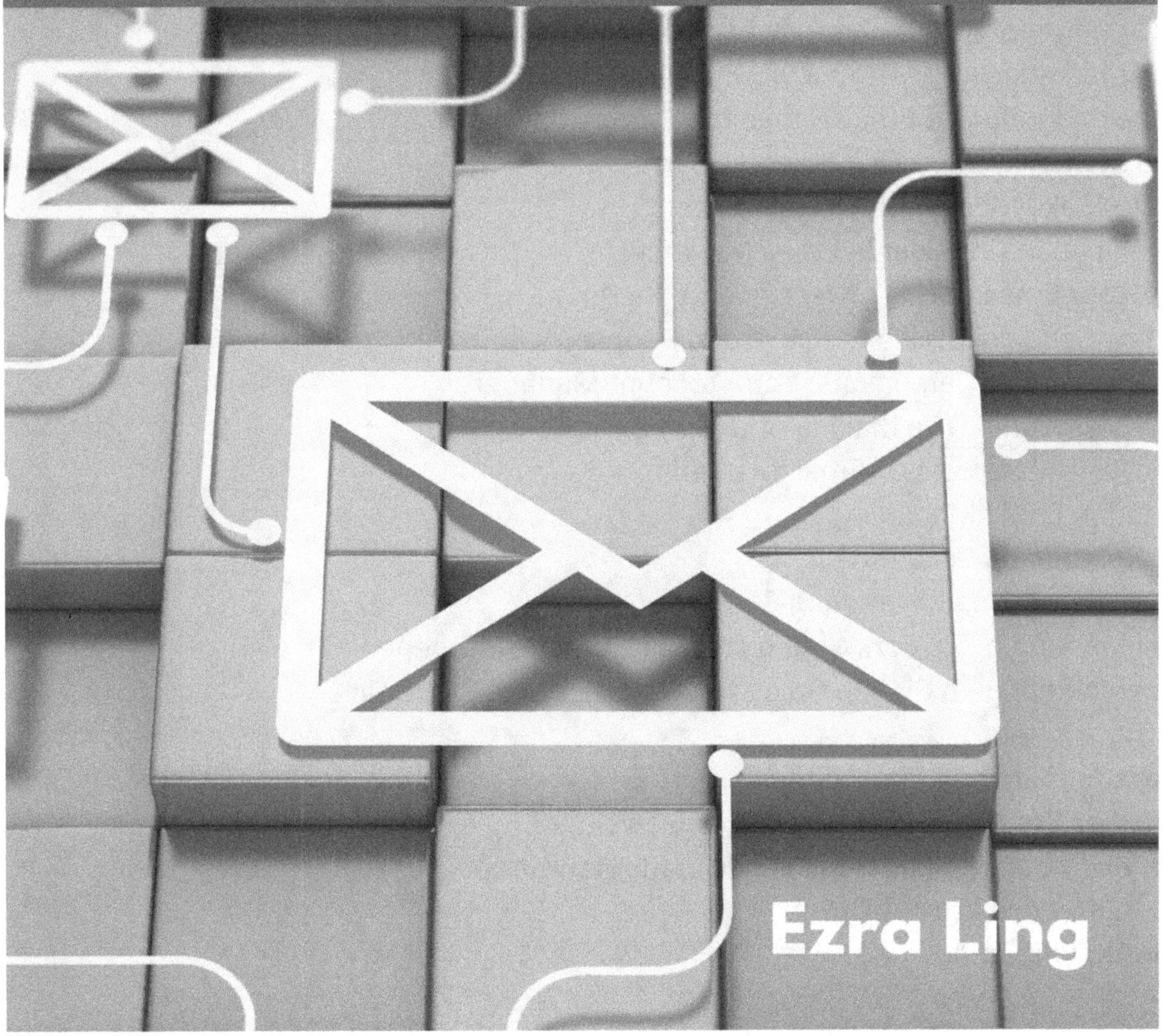

Ezra Ling

Table of Contents

Email Marketing!

Email Marketing -- It's Hidden Power
How An Email Marketing Campaign Works -- Step By Step
Crafting A Winning Subject Line
Why You Shouldn't Buy Into the Myth of Bulk Email Marketing
More Attention Equals More Business
What are Optin Lists and How Do They Work?
How to Make an Email Marketing Campaign A Success
Four Ways To Capture Email Addresses
Email Etiquette: An Old Strategy But Effective For New Products
Email Marketing - The Groundwork
Unique and Valuable Email Marketing Campaigns
Email Marketing: Use This Powerful Tool
How to Make Money With a Newsletter
Five Things to Consider in Email Marketing
Keep Your Emails Short, Direct, and to the Point
Are You Sending Emails to the Wrong People?
Email Marketing Campaigns: Your Account Manager
Email Marketing - The Making of a Marketing Campaign
Discover The Secrets Of Email Marketing
Mastering Email Marketing
Why Companies Send Emails
The Secret of Email Marketing Success: Giving!
Email Marketing: Tips on Writing an Email That Gets Opened
Email Marketing - A Simple Guide to Writing Emails That Deliver
One Time Offers
5 Ways to Build a Valuable Email List
4 Tips For Creating a Highly Effective Newsletter
How Much Content Should I Include in My Newsletter?
How to Improve Your Skills?
Using Double Opt In

Email Marketing Tips

SEO & Affiliate Marketing!

How to Make Money With Affiliate Programs
Affiliate Marketing - 4 Factors to Consider When Looking For a Product
Dealing With Affiliate Partners
Online Affiliate Marketing: The Battle Cry
How to Get More Clicks to Your Affiliate Products
Why Pay for Affiliate Marketing?
Do You Want to Get Results Fast Or Slowly?
Keeping Track Of Your Progress
Why Online Purchasing is Popular
Get Online Video Marketing Up and Running
A Guide To Video Marketing
Search Engine Optimization - New and Relevant Traffic!
Control Quality - Stop Trying to Get Instant Results in Your Marketing
Marketing Strategies: A Way of Being Advertised
Affiliate Marketing: How To Build Your List Using Social Media?
Affiliate Marketing: 3 Ways To Be Successful
Tips To Improve Your Website
How To Make Emails With Affiliate Products More Effective
What You Should Know About Blogging and How to Use t
Is Your Blog Operating On All Foundations?
How to Make Your Blog's Content Fresh and Relevant
Advertise Your Business With a Story
Busy Busy Busy -- Stop!
Top Time Management Tips - Don't be a Slave to Your Phone
Search Engine Optimization -- The Secret To Online Profits
Top 5 Blogging Tips
Learn These 5 Skills to Become a Real Millionaire Entrepreneur

Introduction

As any internet marketer worth their salt would tell you, you should never underestimate the power of email marketing. So if you don't know what's the best marketing tool you're looking for, I suggest you **start building a list!** It might end up being the most powerful tool you have for building your business and making money online.

What makes email marketing so powerful? When it comes to building a profitable online business, email marketing is a cheap, personal, and direct means of connecting with your customers and growing your business. Even big companies rely heavily on email marketing to deliver products or set appointments. With so much room for creativity, email marketing is still a center of innovation. The goal is to create a powerful list of subscribers and target them with emails with an intuitive email design and layout that represent and embody the essence of your brand. Simple is often better in email marketing.

Email marketing is by no means outdated. Even the largest corporations know the power of email marketing. A key difference between email and let's say, paid advertising, is that email is personal. This distinction is pivotal in understanding the dynamics of email marketing. Nobody will likely even open your email unless they're vaguely interested.

Thus, successful email marketing campaigns must appeal to people in a personal and direct way, which is why the **power of attraction** or the feminine principle is so pivotal for success. At the same time, the masculine principle is just as important, representing the **numbers game and perseverance aspect** of email marketing. But, you must stay consistent with your brand's identity. The power of attraction is the art of making your emails so attractive and appealing, almost magnetizing, that people will open them, dig them, and wait for the next one.

Email marketing is also a number's game. You must keep improving all aspects of your game. Technical knowledge and implementation is important as well, like creating HTMLs or creating filters to separate contacts with high response rates from colder leads. The good news, unlike pretty-much every other form of marketing such as traditional media or sales letters, you have complete control over your email campaign! A successful email campaign is a perfect opportunity to bond with your customers.

To begin with, you are able to personalize your emails. You get to address the people on your list as you choose, and that makes them feel like they're part of a one-on-one relationship with you. As you build a relationship with them, they'll trust you more, and you'll be able to keep them tuned in to your emails! So, with this kind of personalization, it's very easy to get the best of both worlds. You get a highly targeted list of people who are interested in and you can build a relationship with them over time while growing your list exponentially. Then you can start promoting your products or services!

Personalization creates a much more powerful campaign. Now, of course, email marketing is no easy feat! It's an internet marketing strategy that integrates lots of functions within a business. Namely, email marketing is a tool that often incorporates several facets of marketing like branding, affiliate marketing, blogging, graphic design, and can also serve many functions like delivering sales funnels, subscription services, memberships, newsletters, products, invoices, confirmations, direct correspondence, file transfers, and much more! Email is becoming the number one way that businesses communicate with their clients.

So, if you're not used to this kind of thing, I suggest you start with free email marketing software. Don't be afraid to research the internet and watch some videos about various email marketing basics, platforms, and software options. We'll get into it more.

You could find a software package that comes with lots of paid features, but you can find good ones that are totally free or very cheap. Content is king for blogging, but delivery is king for email marketing. That's not to say that content isn't important, but email is a shorter form of communication, hence it needs clear messaging. Autoresponders and automation sequences are also very effective tools for building a profitable list and most-importantly, for getting sales.

The first thing you want to do when you get free email marketing software is to set up your goal for your campaign. In this goal you're able to specify the number of subscribers you want, the length of your campaign, and even the number of emails you're going to send. It's very important that you set this up right from the start! Otherwise, you're going to be wasting your time. This is particularly important if you already have subscribers, contacts, or a business.

But if you set it up right, and you know how many emails you're going to send, and how long your campaign will be, and the number of subscribers, then the next thing you're going to want to do is write your emails!

Writing emails is another thing that calls for a lot of practice! Before you start writing your emails, you should know how your list works, you should know how to address people! You should be able to see things from the receiver's point of view! This is very important if you want to build a powerful relationship! Always write in an email as if you're speaking directly to the person in a conversational style. We'll get into that more.

Once you have your goal set, you can start writing your emails! It's a very important task, because you have to make it seem effortless. And when you build a strong relationship that flows easily, you're building a profitable list!

The thing about email marketing campaigns that sets it apart from other forms of marketing is the fact that you're able to **send your emails out to a huge number of subscribers at once!** You're able to send out your campaign to your list using multiple emailing services! This is a powerful tool, and it's something that most companies don't take advantage of. You have to be able to make decisions quickly, and once you know how to set up your campaign, it's easier to write a campaign!

You see, writing an email campaign is a lot like writing a novel, a very very short novel. You've got to write an excellent story to approach your customers. It's not like writing a blog or posting a content page where you just type it up and click send. That's easy! But writing an email campaign? That's like storytelling. You must set the stage for your products.

So you've seen the benefits of creating an email campaign, right? And there's a couple of reasons why you might want to do this. First of all, you've got some nice looking emails that you've created. And another reason why you might want to do this is because you want to build a relationship with your list!

Disclaimers:

1. This book is accurate and true to the best of the author's knowledge. Content is for informational or entertainment purposes only and does not substitute for personal counsel or professional advice in business, financial, legal, or technical matters.
2. This content is accurate and true to the best of the author's knowledge and is not meant to substitute for formal and individualized advice from a qualified professional.
3. This content reflects the personal opinions of the author. It is accurate and true to the best of the author's knowledge and should not be substituted for impartial fact or advice in legal, political, commercial, or personal matters.
4. This content is intended for enlightenment purposes only.

(Blank Page)

Email Marketing!

1. Email Marketing - It's Hidden Power

Email marketing is the name given to a form of direct marketing by email. Most marketers consider it to be very successful compared to other methods of marketing. The reason for this is that emails that are sent through this method are very effective. It can be sent to millions of recipients within seconds. It can reach its customers whenever a marketer wishes. It is less expensive and much faster than any other means of marketing.

Email marketing is the best way to deliver **newsletters, direct marketing messages, special promotions, ezines, announcements, offers, attachments, and invoices to clients at the same time and much more!** This is the reason why email marketing is highly regarded by the largest corporations. It would seem that these companies would find a way of evolving past email marketing, but no. This is what makes it so great. It's extremely diverse in the way it can be used. But, there are several drawbacks with this method of marketing as well. There are advertisers who use this method to send unsolicited emails to their potential customers. People who misuse this method can end up in the spam folder or banned off the server altogether. This is not very effective. It is also very annoying to the recipients. **Any great instrument can be misused in the wrong hands.**

The main goal of email marketing is to sell services and products to a certain group of people who want to know more about the services or products. This group of people can be a group of prospects, who want to know more about the services or products. If the marketer has good relationships with their clients, then they should be able to sell the products or services very well.

In order to send emails to your potential clients, you can use free mailing list software. This should provide you all the features that you will need in order to send the email to your potential clients. You should be provided with all the data that you will need like the name of the people that have requested information and their email address.

You can use a mailing list software to send the messages to the group of people in bulk. You can send the messages to the group of people in multiple formats like HTML, plain text, and rich text. If done correctly, the recipients will not be able to tell that the message that they will receive is coming from a list marketing software, in most cases. This way, they will not be able to see the sender's details unless they have a way to uncover it. If the message arrived in a plain text format, they will in most cases not be able to see the sender's name or form field.

Five Things To Get Started With Email Marketing

You need to have very clear objectives, a plan and follow up in order for you to have a successful campaign. Here are five key things to remember before you get started in your email marketing campaign.

1. Focus: The most important thing is to make sure you have your objectives in order. Do you want to get customers to open your emails or just get them to click on the links? Will your customers get raving responses or just a few? What emotion are they designed to trigger? What are your ultimate objectives and how will you be measuring results?

2. Plan: Remember to always have a plan of action. Figure out how often you will email your customers or how you will email them. Will you email once a month, bi-weekly or once a week, or more? What is the timing of your emails; do you want to email at specific intervals or will one particular day or time be best?

3. Format: Use a format that is easy for people to read. Remember to make your format easy on the eyes and not too busy or graphic-heavy. Make sure the format and design of the email is a good representation of your brand.

4. Content: Always keep the content of your emails relevant to your main objectives. Always be looking for any way you can to increase the effectiveness of your emails. This could be by re-working the content or by using some graphics that are not too common and will increase the effect of the email.

5. Follow up: Make sure you follow up well. Never send emails to people that you do not know well or have no intention to connect with.

By keeping these key things in mind you can ensure the success of your campaign. Remember: don't go in blind, get them to click on your links and give rave responses.

Setting Goals In Email Marketing

In order to achieve your goals, you must have a target. I'm sure you've heard this before, but for some people it might be something along the lines of, "I want to increase my sales." But what exactly is your weakest link that is affecting sales? What is it that generates more value or interest for the customer? Constantly improving your weakest areas as a marketer, whether it is gathering a quality list, cleaning up your emails, or using a story to approach your customers, is crucial for success.

Everyone is aware of the fact that it gets harder over time to get even the smallest bit of income out of a product. If you constantly keep improving the product, then the inefficiencies are gradually removed, leaving an end product and process that has reached its full potential for generating sales. **However, the beauty of email marketing is that you can always expand your email list or switch up the design of the email itself, without changing the secret sauce on the product's end!** Not everyone is aware of how much harder that task is if you're generating sales through a traditional pipeline like a retail location or even an online shop.

The fact of the matter is, people buy products, not ideas. Not strategies. Not secrets. For the most part, people buy products and services which are associated with a certain emotion or problem. So, people buy products because they either have a problem, or because they have an emotion driving them to buy something.

Different emotions drive people to buy different products. For example, insurance is often sold through the emotion of fear (of loss), luxury cars are sold through the emotion of privilege, and vacations are sold with the emotion of "escaping the daily grind" or recouping. This is not a judgemental statement, simply an observation.

So, in order to increase sales, you have to get the mindset of trying to solve a problem of the buyer or get in tune with their wavelength on an emotional level. You must understand what is driving your customers to make the purchases that they do.

Understanding Your Audience

In order to understand and align with your audience, you must consider:

- What problem are they trying to solve?
- What emotion is motivating them?
- What do they want to avoid in dealing with this problem or emotion?
- What do they consider as the ideal outcome?

Just as understanding your customers and subscribers is important, don't be afraid to build your lists. The more prospects you have on your list, the more likely you are going to get more responses and hopefully, sales.

The goal of building your lists is to have a 'base' of prospects you can market to in a far more efficient and effective manner. The rest is icing on the cake. The best way to do this is by making it easy for them to opt-in to your list. This way they are going to know what they are getting into and the level of risk they are willing to take in subscribing. It also gives you the opportunity to target a much more specific audience by adding other subscribers who have also opted into your lists and by refining your lists.

The Importance of Building a List

Building your lists takes time, but it is essential. It is important to have a 'base' of prospects that you can market to from day one, so you will be able to set your 'autoresponder' to send out messages on a 'daily or near daily basis.

The key to understanding your audience is to know what they like and react to, what motivates them to give up information about themselves. The easiest way to do this is to ask them, make it easy for them to tell you what they like and react to. Remember that the goal of building your lists is to use it to target each subscriber with the offer that will be the best fit for them.

What is important is to make sure that you are able to deliver your emails consistently and use the right vocabulary and wording in your emails. We want to sell without seeming pushy, though, some persistence is required. You should always make sure you have a regular 'unsubscribe' link on all of your emails. This gives you an opportunity to test whether your emails are given consent by allowing the subscriber the option to opt-out.

Learn from every small success. Be creative in 'gold-plating' any links you have in your emails to improve the chances that they will be seen and clicked on. Also, avoid words like "buy" or "make a purchase" as these activate negative or defensive triggers in people's minds.

While most people actually want to spend money, they don't want to think of it as expenditure. Hence, instead using a phrase like "ready to make a purchase?" you can use something like "let's move forward!" or "let's get the paperwork out of the way" or "secure your new [fill in the black]." In addition, instead of using the word "contract," it's better to use "agreement" which is less binding on a psychological level.

In summary, the importance of email lists with an unsubscribe option is to avoid spamming people with emails that won't get opened, hurting your sender ratings, and making it more likely for your emails to end up in the spam folder. Rather, deliver the best message possible to the people who are on your email list who are interested in hearing you out.

Email marketing is the latest craze among the business elite who have finally woken up to the power of marketing through emails. The emails have been delivered to every conceivable address in the land in what has been termed as "The Internet Wholesale Revolution". This is the time when email marketing has gone from a sideshow to a main business asset and businesses are beginning to realise the benefits of email marketing!

If done correctly, it can result in the business totally cutting out the middleman by getting right in front of its customers in a matter of seconds. This is a great advantage but it requires a little bit of skill to manage the marketing campaign appropriately.

Companies are using HTML in their emails in order to make them more appealing to customers. They are changing the links to hyperlinks, moving around the text and replacing it with pictures and music. HTML is a really great technology but it also means that the emails get too large and too many people will get sick of reading them. In many situations, HTML emails are so much better than ordinary text emails. Avoid overdoing, however, as this may result in your emails getting flagged and redirected to the spam folder. You could try installing special plugins to your email account to aid in creating a professional-looking HTML email if that feature isn't already available.

Recap: the email marketing company should be able to manage the campaign appropriately and be able to deliver a quality product. The company should be able to use a format that is easy to read and understand. The system should deliver the messages in a fashion that makes it easy for the customer to unsubscribe by giving an unsubscribe link on the email.

2. How An Email Marketing Campaign Works -- Step By Step

Someone has subscribed to your mailing list. They click on a link to receive further information about your products or services. They are given a link to confirm that they really do want to receive further information from you. This is also where they are given the chance to change their email address. This way, you are able to maintain a clean mailing list that nobody else can access. You are able to remove addresses from the list that unsubscribe at their request. You are also able to keep track of where your clients are located geographically. This allows you to send information to people that are located in a specific geographic area. This allows you to send targeted information to people that are likely interested in your products and services.

These are examples of how email marketing works. The important part is that the client has provided their data to you. This is where you can market your products and services using email marketing.

Designing Email Sequences (Prior to Contact Segmentation)

The **first email** marketing campaign you should consider using is a welcome email. This email is sent when a customer has opted in or confirmed their interest in receiving further information from you. In this welcome email you should mention the date and time of your next email campaign. You should also explain what benefits there will be for customers and how long your email will be sent. You should also state that you will periodically send an announcement email as well. Also mention that you will send regular updates and that they can unsubscribe at any time.

This email is also sent to people who have specified that they do not want to receive further emails. In this case you should send a special message thanking them for their interest and offering to cancel or remain subscribed to the email newsletter.

The **second email** marketing campaign you should consider using as an 'Update'. In this you should send an explanation of any new products or services that you have launched. You should also state that you will send weekly updates, a reminder to buy or contact your sales department for more information.

The **third email** marketing campaign is where you present the "direct offering" or "meat" of your offer. Introduce your customers to your products and services, and be direct in your offering. This is a chance to get customers on board that are already primed to make a purchase, as well as set the stage for those on the fence. You should try to include visual elements like images or moving elements with colors to entice customers to make a purchase or a commitment.

The **fourth email** marketing campaign you should consider using is for updates and news. In this email you should explain what is new in your product range. Also mention any current discounts you are offering. In this email you should also try to convince people to 'forward to a friend' if they haven't already done so. You should also offer a 'sign up to our newsletter' link if people have not done so already.

The **fifth email** marketing campaign you should consider using is an 'urgent'. In this you should remind customers of upcoming events or competitions. You should also remind customers of any upcoming sales or discounts. Also in this campaign you should explain what your recent special offers are. Also mention what customers can expect from you in future emails.

The **sixth email** marketing campaign you should consider using is for feedback. In this you should ask customers about their experiences using your products or services. Also ask for suggestions and any further information they may require. In this case you should also explain your recent policies and explain what they can expect to see from you. Also ask for unsubscribing requests.

The **seventh email** marketing campaign you should consider using is for 'informational'. In this you should ask customers to send you any feedback or questions they may have. You should also explain how they can receive a copy of your newsletter or website. Also explain what they can expect to see in future emails. You should consider all these steps and guidestones when you send in your email marketing campaigns. Also, it's wise to keep in mind that customer behaviour often differs from what you would like them to do. So always consider that not all customers are interested in what you are offering them.

3. Crafting A Winning Subject Line

The subject line of the email is the first thing that your recipients see. It is here that they can make the decision whether to open your email or delete it. So it is important to write a subject line that grabs their attention and causes them to take action.

Writing a good subject line can be tricky because if you don't do it right then it can be the only thing your recipients remember about the email. There is no point in wasting valuable email space showing a familiar message to be bad, so make sure you understand what will compel them to take action, such as providing them with something of value (great suggestion, new information, a discount offer, etc.).

There are three phases to your subject line, and each of them will be described here.

1. Build interest

If your subject line works on its own to get people to open the email, then this is the phase where you should make your offer work with an added incentive or threat. This is probably the easiest to do. Here you should always use words such as "free" or "special" to build interest and make them open the email.

2. Make the reader take action

This is the most difficult phase. This is where you tell them what to do. For example if your offer is a free report or newsletter then you can use "download the free report" or "get the special report now" to get them to take action. You can also include words such as "now", "tomorrow", "tomorrow night", "your way", etc. to direct them to a particular place or action. For example: "Don't miss our next workshop on Wednesday at 7pm".

3. Tell them how they can do something

Now you are telling them what to do. It is here that you can tell them to register for a webinar, join a list, subscribe to a newsletter, purchase a product, etc. This is where you show them the actual path that should help them to get the action they want.

After you have completed all three phases you are ready to send an email. Remember that you can always build interest in the third phase, but this is often just not possible. The idea is to prime your email list without sounding repetitive, redundant, or too pushy. You want to find the perfect balance of friendly and down-to-business.

Making It Easy For Customers to Interact With You

- The products and services must be a good fit for your customers. If you are offering innovative products and services, then make sure they don't create new problems in your customer's lives! Technical errors or failed designs may create a sense of long-term dissatisfaction and soon enough most people are in a mindframe of "dealing" with customers rather than building positive relationships with them. In order to avoid unwanted problems, make sure your products and services are strategic assets for your customers, not temporary solutions.

- It's easy to interact with your customers and deliver the products and services. If the product and services you are offering is not an easy job, then don't wait for them to call you. Give the information about the products and services that are in line with their requirements. So, you must be very careful about the details that you are providing to the customers. When you give such detailed information then there is a greater chance that they will communicate with you.

- It must be convenient for them. Their life must be convenient for them. Because they are in a hurry. It must be easy for them to go to the websites, to make purchases, and to interact with your organization. It must be convenient for them to order the products and services that you are offering. It must be convenient for them to receive their products and services and ask for assistance.

In the world of internet marketing, you need to keep track of emails you have sent out in order to sort the good from the bad and to get the ones that have gone bad.

4. Why You Shouldn't Buy Into the Myth of Bulk Email Marketing

Basically every single email business knows that the ultimate aim of the email marketing campaign is a) customer interaction in the form of a purchase and b) a relevant exchange of information or messages with the correct recipients to ensure a long-term relationship.

Today, it's worth stating again that the ideal scenario of marketing campaigns is the one where the emails in question are sent to the right people and for the right reason. The current scenario involves not only the idea that email marketing should be used to build relationships and trust with customers, but also that these messages need to be delivered at the right time with the right underlying emotion. While bulk outreach is certainly a major advantage of email marketing, you must ensure good practices are kept so that the quality of your leads is not diminished.

Email marketing campaigns involve several drafting stages:

1. Planning. The planning starts long before the actual launch of the email marketing campaign. The key part of the process is the task of identifying the recipients that would be most likely to be people who are going to want the product or service that you are going to offer.

2. Selecting. The recipient list is selected based on the list of intended recipients (most likely buyer's list). The best choice of recipients is also determined by an analysis of their buying pattern.

3. Research. The content of the emails is assessed based on what kind of content is needed and how it will be delivered. For example, if you plan to publish text emails, then the emails should be brief, precise, short, sweet, smart, useful, informative, elegant, and attractive. The emails need to be written in simple words and made elegant. You can do research on the market to know the customers' needs.

4. Pre-launch. The content of the email messages is also composed. The time of the launch is planned. The recipients are selected based on their buying patterns and the content is designed to be relevant to the recipient's buying pattern.

It's the final stage of the email marketing campaign process that is critical. The recipients are selected based on the recipients' buying pattern and their interest in the product offering. In addition, the recipient is selected according to their past buying behavior. Based on the history of the customer, the type of campaigns they are sending, and the product offering, the best possible recipients are selected.

What is The Best Email Marketing Strategy?

The truth is, there is no ONE recipe for scaling your online business using email marketing. Rather, there are many different strategies and you must test each strategy in the market to see if it works for your niche. Playing the numbers game with bulk email marketing may work for your niche if your level of customization for each product is relatively low, but it may not work for other niches. It's hard to predict with many factors at play, which is why trial-and-error is so important when doing email marketing. The best email markers allow for a certain margin of randomness to discover new insights about their customers and target audience. **The one thing to remember is that you want to avoid exhausting your readers with too many emails, particularly if they have little entertainment value. If you plan on sending lots of emails, make them interesting to read by adding snippets of interesting information or statistics to go along with your offer.**

Now, many will tell you to use nothing but proven marketing strategies, and in a recent study, the opt-in email marketing technique came out on top for generating sales. While it took the top spot, the majority of marketers have abandoned the proven marketing strategies, in favour of the other methods such as PPC and blog marketing, in order to get more targeted traffic. However, **email marketing is proving its effectiveness over and over again.**

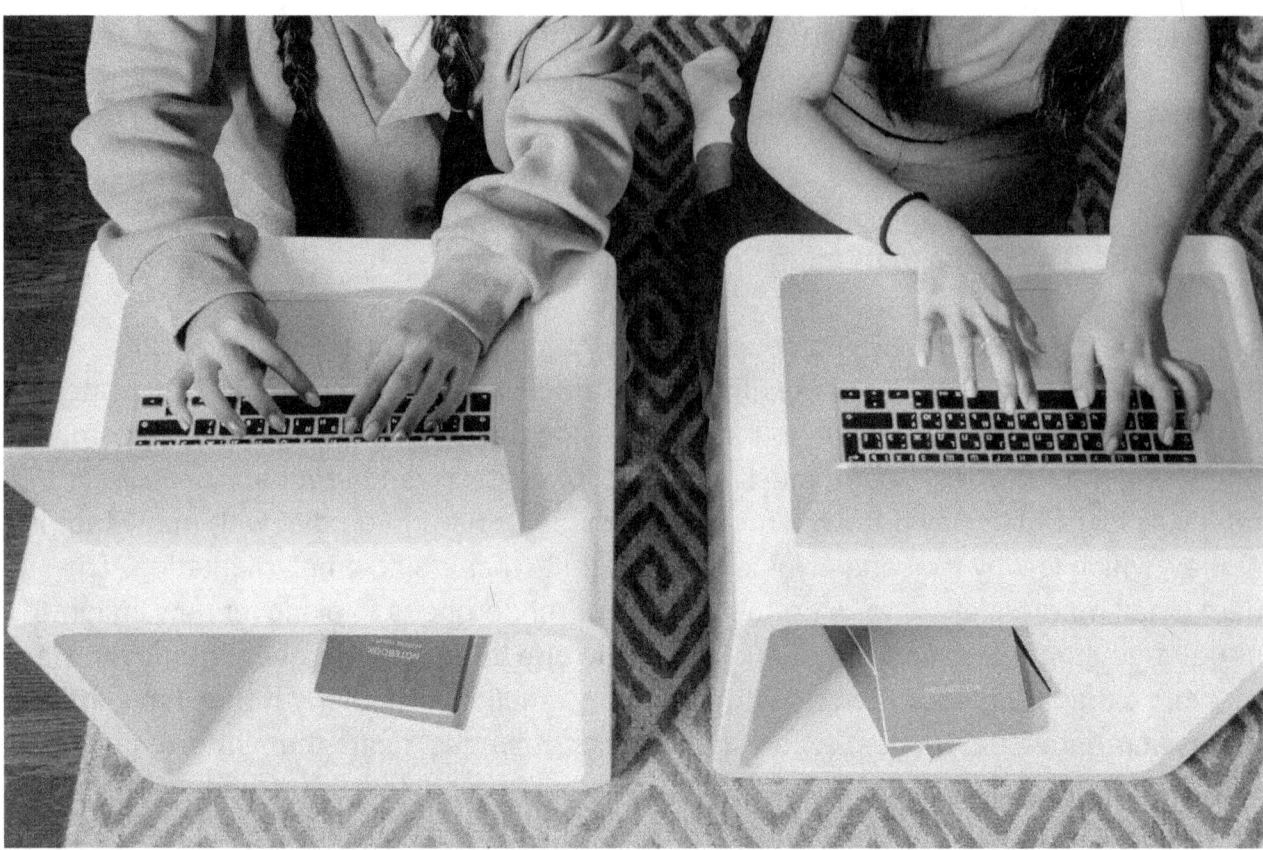

While creating a responsive email list may require some time and resources, it's well worth it in most cases. Once you have a list, you can keep promoting new offers down the same pipeline and if the target audience is right, you're bound to make sales with every campaign.

1. Develop a good relationship with your website visitors and subscribers

This is the first step in developing a good relationship with your visitors, so that they will open your emails, look forward to your emails, and read your emails over again. So your email marketing strategy must build on a strong relationship already established with your website visitors.

2. Develop a good relationship with your social network followers.

This is important as your social network followers will likely be the biggest buyers on your list. If you ever want to reach the largest possible number of buyers on your list, **you need to develop a strong relationship with them**. As well as that, you want to make sure your content is relevant to them. So don't make promises you cannot keep, or content that is irrelevant to them. Don't just target your mailing list, but target your followers on all your social network channels also. Storytelling is a great method of "unveiling" your brand. Create protagonists in your stories that resemble your customers and introduce antagonists or problems that are similar to those that your customers face. Demonstrate how your products or services solved the protagonist's problems. Powerful or just funny stories can be used on social media to promote your brand and achieve rapid growth on social networks.

3. Develop a good relationship with forum users.

Another way to promote your products is by simply promoting your products on forums. And in order to make sure that you get the most from forums, develop a good relationship with the forum users and keep promoting your products. Your relationship with the forum community is your key to a very profitable commerce. In order to do this, you must always be very honest and promote products with the truth in mind. And to promote honesty, it's best to get a paid membership on forums, as many of the paid memberships will often also act as a filter and keep your content from being deleted and make sure your emails get a higher open rate.

Building a list through email marketing is not as easy as it may seem. It's not simply about sending an email, and then waiting for your list to grow. The truth is it takes an awful lot of work just to get a list. The more work you put into building your email list, the bigger your list can grow. So be honest and work really hard to grow your email list.

If you have not already done so, create a good relationship with your list members, for example by sending them an email everyday and simply letting them know how fantastic your products are and how they can use them. Or, tell them how great THEY are! And, if you can offer a free download to your list as well, then do so. **The truth is that a good download helps to build a relationship, and creates interest in your products and your business. This brings us to another pivotal point. Make people feel special. People like to feel special. Find ways to make people feel like they are receiving special treatment. This could be done in the form of special access, special discounts, special perks, special features, etc.**

Plus, sending bulk emails without diligently collecting a good list can hurt your sender status, resulting in your emails being forwarded to spam folders. In addition, buying random email lists is not a good strategy for many reasons. What's important to know now is that sending in bulk is no problem, if you have properly obtained your email list through an opt-in or subscription form filled out by the individual. This gives you the permission to keep emailing them, provided they have the ability to opt out and do not explicitly ask you to stop.

5. More Attention Equals More Business

When you have the attention of the masses, you can make money. If you have traffic that does not arrive at your website, you may find yourself without an online business and a lot of money. That is just plain annoying. Not only that, you are losing money to the automatic senders. Generating traffic is difficult to begin with, so make sure to collect email information from visitors using signup forms. These lists become your goldmine. Once you have the list, you can think about autoresponders and campaigns.

The first thing you should think about is that you are doing this for the money. Not because you are doing it just for the fun of it. Traffic of any quality will often help you make money if you can get people to your website and sign up for the newsletter. In time, they can bring you additional income. These visitors can also bring you some additional sales of other products you sell to them. Once you have a list that brings in sales of products and services, you may find yourself with a nice income.

As with any internet business, it is very likely that you will need to take some action to keep the money rolling in. You can use some of the techniques mentioned in this segment to do just that. **As I always like to say, email marketing is a medium-term endeavour as far as CRM (customer relationship management) is concerned. Sometimes, this can change depending on the type of niche and company you are. Generally, the rule of thumb is, the more higher-end or more expensive your products or services are, the longer the CRM timeframe is.**

You're not necessarily building lifetime clients because at some point, your offerings can get exhausted, but you are not doing this for the short-term either. It takes time to earn trust from customers. You can continue to offer them information on the topic that they like to keep the ball rolling. Sometimes, a subscriber won't purchase anything from you but still enjoy the newsletter. That too is an asset.

When customers do not consider you as spammer, they are more likely to continue buying from you, consuming more content, and directly contributing to more business. If you make them feel important, they should feel that you are giving them something worthwhile and as a result, will often continue to buy from you and even share your content. When you are sending emails on a regular basis, you will probably become more familiar to your readers. You should be able to communicate more in your emails and feel that they are thinking of you as well. In the long run, if you do it right, many will even begin to like you. As they realize that you are a real person and feel like they are talking to a friend, they should continue to treat you as a friend and respond to your emails as well.

As mentioned above, there are several email marketing software programs that are out there that you can buy. There are some that you can build your own package from the ground up with your own features and preferences and packages that can be hired out. **As the name implies, hired out means that the service is based on cost and volume.** The price is based on the number of emails that are sent in a month and the size of your list. The service also gives you the choice of how many or how few they want to send to your list. But, it's better to learn and do it in-house since email marketing will likely become a cornerstone of your business in due time.

One of the features of advanced software is the built in database that it comes with. This can be used to look back at your history of e-mails and your history of users. It can give you analytics about your subscribers like demographics in addition to other data, including when they subscribed and unsubscribed, how often they open your emails, for how long, and other statistical information. This information can be very helpful when you are sending out follow-up messages. That's because it will help you to discern the best way to approach them. In addition, people who unsubscribe may be interested in your product but not necessarily in the newsletter you are sending out to them.

Once you have configured your database settings and other settings like notifications, you can then send your emails out. There are also a lot of programs out there that are "autoresponders" that will allow you to create emails in advance and have them sent out in the future at a set time. The software varies in price but the best programs are the ones that you will build from the ground up with yourself in mind. You also want to make sure you are not limited by the number of emails you can send out each month.

You can then customize autoresponders according to your needs and then install them on your own domain name and make them work for you. When you are getting an autoresponder, it should be able to create both HTML and plain text emails. It should also have a spam checker. These are essential because many people will put any type of ad in their emails. If it gets flagged as spam, then you can get an automatic response saying so. You should make sure that if you do use an autoresponder that you do not insert dead links in your emails because this can get you blacklisted in certain ISPs. In order to avoid this, set a link in the email and if there is a dead link, simply click the link and remove it.

Finally, organizing your contacts and their information is crucial for dissecting how to target each group of contact in the best way. Your product or service may have a broad target audience or subscriber list, so you should organize and filter your contact information in a way that lets you dictate how to segment them into email lists.

Once you have subscribers who are willing to share information, you have them as contacts whose information is neatly organized, then segment them into separate email lists before designing a campaign that strategically targets said email list. In other words, instead of sending out emails to all of your contacts, try to segment them by age, loyalty, geography, income, etc depending on the circumstances. In time, you'll have a better grasp of how to segment your contact list to best your sales. And remember, you can judge successful segmentations based on several markers, such as open rate, average duration of read-time, link click-through rate, or call-to-action rate.

6. What are Optin Lists and How Do They Work?

If you've been online for any length of time, you've heard the expression 'opt in'. It is often used when talking about subscriber lists. This means you are offering something in exchange for your subscriber or customer's email address. The more you can get away with asking your subscribers to give you their names and email addresses in return for receiving newsletters and offers on your products or services, the higher the ratio of opt-ins you will get. Thus, your subscriber or customer list can grow exponentially. However, you cannot add a new subscriber unless they have explicitly signed up or opted in to receive mail from you.

Your subscriber list is the true 'cash cows' of your business. A quality list is virtually just as important as a quality campaign. Both are crucial elements. If your list is out-dated, or even worse, ridden with false emails, your server may refuse to execute your campaign! Ouch! Hence, a good email list is the true money tree and you must build it. The list is the true fruit from the tree of your online business. Without it, you are just a peddler selling fruit, not a farmer growing crops.

So, we now know where our email address comes from. Now, we need to add what is known as 'opt out' and the process becomes clear. Let's take the example of the car salesman. He is selling a car and wants to collect email addresses from new customers. He knows that most people prefer to buy the car before they part with their email address and e-mail addresses are the only way he can reach them. So, he offers a deal with a buy now or buy later option.

The new customer then opts in and the salesman can send them information about any specials he is running or offering, his website link, the way to get financing or lease, his contact information etc.

As you can see, opt in lists can be extended into the many hundreds, thousands and even millions. It is what the internet marketers term a 'goldmine' in the online world. What you need to be a successful online entrepreneur is a list building approach. And the number one ingredient in list building is 'list growth'. You see, the biggest problem online business owners face is their lists. It is the real Achilles heel of many internet marketers.

But, you need to see your list building as a business, not a hobby. And the number one way you can grow your list is with a **'free offer'.** Let's say you want to build a list of 20,000 subscribers. You don't need to spend a cent. You can just make a 'free offer'. It's as simple as that. You can create content for free for starters and then offer it for free in your newsletters. Then, after your subscribers are trained by your free offer, you can offer an affiliate product that costs them a few dollars, or hundreds, or even thousands. The free offer could even be a coupon for savings off a purchased product or service. For example, "click here to receive $100 in savings off your next purchase!"

Now for the problem. Most people are hesitant to give away their contact information if the free giveaway is seen as marketing material. Well guess what? **Give away something that's actually valuable! There's no reason why you should be hoarding in your giveaway. If you don't know what to give, think of a free discount, book, seminar, webinar, how-to content, free visitation, etc. It doesn't have to cost you lots of money**

just for it to be free! So you build your list by creating giveaways. Take advantage of the fact that people like free. When they are ready to sell, you then market your products. In other words, you are training them to be a customer and that is the purpose of your giveaway opt-in lists.

With the list of people who are ready to buy, you can then market your products. Your goal is to have a list of people who want to buy and you can market and sell products and services that your business can offer. You should know that you are in business to build a list of buyers. And you can keep growing your list of buyers and, when it is time to sell, you can build a list of buyers who want to buy.

Email marketing is a method of internet marketing which allows you to sell your product without having to physically go to your customer and sell it in person. Instead, you send the product to your customers by email if it is digital, or you send it by post and send an order confirmation by email. As the name implies, email marketing is a form of direct marketing which sends email to a targeted list of people. This form of marketing could be linked with phone numbers, but is not reliant upon it. There are many benefits of this type of marketing which entails the ability to reach any subscriber on a global scale instantly. Autoresponders allow you to send perfectly-timed emails in bulk without huge labor fees as in phone marketing operations.

When considering the benefits of using this type of fast-paced yet methodical marketing strategy, your main concern should be the growth of your business through the quality of the email lists. In order to ensure this, relevant information and giveaways must be offered during opt-in campaigns. There are several companies who are currently offering these services to various people but you should look for a company that will offer you the best services possible. Of course, there are other benefits associated with email marketing. Among these other benefits are cost savings which can be a big advantage for you if you are in the business of selling products.

When considering the benefits of this type of marketing you must remember that when sending an email to your customers they are not in an online environment. There is something that is called in email marketing, an opt in email list. When a customer subscribes to an opt-in email list they are added to a list of email addresses that you have either purchased or you have gathered yourself.

Recap

An opt-in email list is a customer's email address list which has been rented from a marketing company or created yourself. Your email list should contain email addresses of customers who have given you permission to send them information about your products. When you send emails to them, they can not only confirm they are interested in hearing about your products but they can also send feedback to you about your emails, your promotions, and anything they think may be of interest to them.

Using an opt-in email list allows you to automate your business instead of manually sending emails to each and every customer you target. With an opt-in email list you can send them one promotional email about your products and then collect their email addresses at a later time when you are ready to send them an email promoting other products. Also, using an opt-in email list makes it much easier to increase the amount of sales that you are making because these customers have already expressed their interest in buying your products.

What is an Autoresponder?

An autoresponder is a tool that is essential in email marketing. An autoresponder will automate the process of sending emails to customers who have opted in to receive emails from you. For example, you have just written an email about your new product and you want to make sure you are sending it to only those customers who are interested in buying your product. It's a good idea to use an autoresponder but don't forget that you should not send it until they have opted into your emails list.

Most autoresponders are already incorporated into your email software/service provider, but often included as a paid upgrade to a free or trial version. Once you get going with sending out lots of emails to a large contact list, you'll want to make the best of your autoresponder because this can save you tremendous time and resources. You can even design how an autoresponder reacts according to an action diagram or decision tree. The best email services have excellent autoresponders that let you automate the process of sending out emails and collecting data. For example, the email list you place a contact into may depend on whether or not they are a returning customer, or depending on their click-through rate of past emails. You want to avoid sending emails to customers that don't open them as this will affect your bounce rate. These are only a few considerations to think through from a plethora of factors to consider when setting up autoresponders.

7. How to Make an Email Marketing Campaign A Success?

Do you want to send more emails to your clients? Are you interested in improving your communication skills? This article contains many useful tips to help you in your email marketing efforts.

Tip #1 - Make Sure to Make Your Email a Single Message

In order for you to get a higher open rate you must ensure that your email is a single message. Single-message emails tend to get higher open rates because they do not have to contend with the effects of images, graphics, HTML, links, etc.

Tip #2 - Avoid or Limit the Use of Flash (unless it is appropriate with your niche or branding)

Flash is a major turning point in email marketing. Once a company uses flash, especially over a long period of time, they will likely become known as a company who uses Flash. This is often a big marketing move. By using flash, your email is destined to become annoying, difficult to read, and also extremely time consuming to open. You must ensure that you do not use flash in your emails. That is the traditional view. However, in some instances, flash can be good for you! It all depends on the type of branding you want for your company, and the niche you're in. For industries where safety is a concern or that entail a high degree of risk, like construction or finance, it's probably better to avoid overly-flashy email designs as this could create a wrong kind of impression for your business.

Tip #3 - Do Not Overpromote

Most people hate being sold to, especially if you come off as being too pushy. When you over promote in your emails, your open rate can suffer. When you provide too much information about your product or service, people can find it difficult to make an investment decision.

Tip #4 - Do Not Let Your Email Become Too Long

When you send too long an email, it can be difficult for people to decide what information they should receive. People also tend to find emails that are too long and difficult to read. If you have an email that is too long, consider creating a pdf version of the email and send that.

This segment contains many helpful tips for improving your email marketing skills. Most of the email marketing campaigns we are involved in should fall into these four categories, and in the following portion, I provide specific ways to improve your email marketing efforts in each of these four categories.

Tip #1 - Give it To them!

For many marketers, the strategy of giving away something for free for new subscribers in their emails is very popular. One idea is to set up a free report. Another is a free audiotape or podcast.

Tip #2 - Deliver on Your Promise!

Most marketers tend to break this one very important rule. They often promise a certain thing, but fail to deliver. The result is that after sending out a campaign, people realize that they have actually been reneged upon. People generally get angry and send back an angry email that speaks of their disappointment and how you have let them down. It is important that you do not repeat the same mistakes of the past. A great place to find free content for your campaign is the web. They have a tremendous amount of very interesting and useful material available.

You might also find that for many topics there are groups of bloggers who have started blogs for the same topic. Many of these bloggers will be happy to let you use their posts and even provide a link for you to your campaign, if your offer sounds appealing to them. So always deliver on your promises if you want to upkeep your reputation. Make sure you do not use too many products or services in your campaign. A good tactic is to use a combination of products and services to offer your potential customers more choices.

8. Four Ways to Capture Email Addresses

There are several ways to capture email addresses. The most common method is to place a form on the main page of your website and have your subscribers fill it out. This works well if your website is simple and doesn't have a lot of content. Also, it is easy to track the success of each email message by seeing who opens your emails and who just clicks on the links within them. Your most loyal subscribers are going to be the ones who are willing to receive your email newsletter.

There are other ways to capture email addresses. This could be a time consuming process but also very effective. These methods are the ones we will discuss here. Let's take a look at some of them:

1. **Web pages:** the most common way to capture the email addresses is to place a form on your website. The form is typically on a web page with a text link in the URL. When a visitor lands on your page they are asked to fill in a form. Sometimes your form is just a hyperlink pointing to another page. The next screen is the one that most marketers are using. They are asking their subscribers to type something and submit the form. Many are asking for an email address. Depending on the country and state you are in, a name is asked instead of an email address. This is so they can match the submitted information with an existing database. You can change the form later to ask for a phone number or other information you may need about the subscriber. The idea is to offer the subscriber an incentive to fill out the form.

2. **Business cards**: there are also ways to capture emails in business cards or e-business cards. You could offer a freebie on your desk as a token of appreciation to the subscriber. You could put the incentive on a business card that is handed to you by a subscriber when they visit your office or wherever you have your office. This can give the subscriber the impression that they are being offered something special, not just another offer. You can also have a card that contains the incentive. In that way, the subscriber feels like the incentive can be useful in some way and not just a form. Likewise, you can send out e-business cards as an attachment in an email.

3. **Mobile phones:** many people view their phones as being a way to capture email addresses from their lapsed mobile subscribers. You can provide a link on your website or newsletter that allows your subscribers to provide their email addresses while they are on their mobile phone. It is a great way to get the information because it's quick and easy. Make sure to follow best practices.

4. **Phone conversations**: you can make phone conversations a good way to ask for email addresses. It is a great way to make a connection with your subscribers and a fun way to communicate. The idea is to make the subscriber feel important and make them like you. You can ask for the first name and email address. It is easier to communicate with someone when you have their information instead of asking them everything when they call.

5. **Web form to complete a purchase (shopping cart).** This one is self-explanatory. Have your customer fill out their email when they reach the shopping cart.

It is your obligation to provide a subscriber with a viable option to opt-in and later to opt-out. This option can typically be on your website, in your emails, or on your newsletter, but should be easy to do.

I personally believe that people like to be talked to in a more informal, casual way than in a business setting. But as I said, that is a personal belief. And I believe that a causal connection is a more powerful connection than a business-like connection. The point is that you will likely need to do this in a post as well as in your email.

The third thing that you need to do is to use the word "you". Again you can do this in a post, but I personally prefer to do this in my email. Again it is important that you get in the habit of using the word "you" in your email. A lot.

Different Modalities and Sequences of Email Marketing

The first thing you need is an email marketing server or platform. This program can help you to create and keep track of a large number of emails. This program can also help you to do marketing on the internet. Having a program with an autoresponder can skyrocket your internet sales, expanding it by leaps and bounds. There's about 5-6 major leading email marketing platforms to choose from: a little research online and you'll have more information about what is the best fit for you. Some have pricing plans depending on the size of your contacts, others bill you based on tiers that allow certain numbers of emails or email campaigns to be sent per month. In other situations, the email functionality may be incorporated into a website builder or another system, but this is probably less preferable unless it is thoroughly equipped with all the features that a stand-alone email marketing platform has. Remember, you may also need access to funnels and landing pages as well as plugins that could go hand-in-hand with your email marketing to create a well-integrated marketing machine.

The next thing you need is an autoresponder. This is a program that can send your emails out on autopilot. This program can help you to stay organized and track an ever increasing list of emails. And in fact, it can help you to do so by tracking your subscriber responses to your emails. You should be able to find out how effective your emails are. Sending out emails by segmenting your contact list is a game of trial and error. You'll need some time to determine how to send emails to maximize their efficiency in terms of achieving objectives. Remember, not all emails have the objective to complete a sale. Some emails are for branding, customer service, file delivery, customer relationship management, or keeping your clients engaged with your offering. It's the same debate as choosing the right parameters to track your conversions. So when marketers track conversions, they know there are many steps ultimately leading to a sale. For example, here is a possible sequence:

Email is delivered to customer's inbox (email bounce rate) ----> Customer opens email (email open rate) -----> Customer clicks on link leading to landing page (click through rate) ----> customer clicks on product and is redirected to product page (product page bounce rate) ----> customer adds product to cart (cart rate) -----> customers goes to cart and completes form and places order (sales conversion rate).

It may seem counterintuitive, but sometimes it's better to measure the performance of an email campaign by using an earlier or intermediary conversion market in the chain rather than the end sales conversion rate as this can help you optimize your campaign. In addition, you should pay attention to all steps in the process to figure out where the bottleneck (hiccup) occurs and try to improve it. For example, you may have an excellent product and email, but if the product page is lacking due to a poor product description, the chain likely will ultimately underperform.

The action of responding to emails or creating sequences or decision trees can usually be done through an autoresponder as well. This is a program that can automatically send your follow up emails. This can be done by having your program send out your emails on autopilot, but the autoresponder can also be used to do follow up emails on autopilot.

Email marketing can be done by setting up an email program in your web server. This can be sent to a large number of people by your email marketing software. It is very important that you get your email marketing programs on your web server.

- Your email marketing software can be used to put ads on various websites. This can help you to stay in contact with your customers. It can be used to offer an incentive for your customers to buy your products and put themselves on the subscriber list

- With your autoresponder, you can send out notifications of new products. This can help you to keep your customers abreast of what is new in your website

- You can make newsletters that should keep your customers informed. These newsletters can be sent to your customers

- **Your autoresponder can be used to help you find the best days and times to send out emails to your customers.** This is very important. You need to know when the best days and times to send emails to your customers are. This can be done by an auto responder

9. **Email Etiquette: An Old Strategy But Effective For New Products**

In the old days you would send your email newsletters out using a regular email program like Outlook or some of the other commercial email programs. For most people though, their email inboxes were not cluttered up with junk mail, and they simply deleted junk mail without even bothering to read it. Well, that is not the way it is any more. In the old days it was not considered polite to send junk mail to anyone who did not know you, or even to send it to people that you did not know personally.

Nowadays, if you send emails to anyone that you do not know personally, it is considered slightly rude. But if you send an email to some friends, or even to people that you have met somewhere, it is not considered rude at all. It is considered inconsiderate not to reply to them, unless you don't know them like that.

For this reason, you have to keep in mind to keep in contact with your customers on a regular basis if you're trying to keep them in the loop about your business's goings-on. This doesn't mean spamming them or sending tons of emails, but the key word is **regular**. You do not want to appear rude by sending them junk emails and not bothering to reply to them, but you want to make sure to be building rapport. For this reason, take unresponsive emails (contacts) off your A list.

When someone has bought from you, he or she almost always wants to hear from you. And, if you can provide new information and advice that can help them in their business, then that is even better. But you need to remember to follow the rules.

For example, if you do an internet search for 'email etiquette' you can often see websites with text ads about how people do not want to send unsolicited emails to others. Chances are you will also find a lot of sites that tell you how to filter your emails and to not send your emails to people that you do not know. These rules are not always followed, so again keep in mind. Sometimes, marketers make intentional spelling errors to bypass getting marked as spam.

Of course, some people ignore the rules completely, and send their emails to strangers and then complain when their software tries to warn them and their system cannot find the email. But others follow the rules, and it just pays to be consistent, and follow the rules, so that you can be on good terms with the law, and your customers.

Here is a list of some terminology that marketers try to bypass to avoid getting into the spam folder. However, if you are operating in an ethical way, which includes sending emails only to people who've given consent to do so, you shouldn't worry too much about these terms. Nonetheless, here's a few of the frequently-used email spam trigger words that email marketers tend to avoid to avoid being labeled as spam:

Free
Act now
Bonus
Buy
Cash
Limited
Luxury
Sales
Remove
Lose

Success
Unlimited
Offer
Order Now
Serious
Urgent
Income
Investment
Open
Promise
Expire
Only
Double your income

In addition, try to avoid these things to decrease your chances of landing in the spam folder:

- Avoid adding RE to subject lines
- Avoid one-word subject lines
- Limit the use of video/flash/JavaScript
- Instead of embedding forms, try linking to them
- Avoid posting entire links, rather link it with a word or phrase
- Avoid exclamation (!) marks in your subject lines

How to Be More Personal and Less Salesy

You want to make sure you don't look like a pushy salesperson. The first thing people think of when they think of you is the sales person, and if your signature is something other than your own, they don't know who you are. They want to know you're a real person, not a salesperson. So when you include your spouse's name, business name, or another one of your family names, use a photo of yourself or a personal message, something so personal that they'll recognize you.

Then when they get to your website, include a link to your personal website. When you include a link in an email, make sure you include it in a relevant email, and that you give the recipient **a reason to click through**. If you have a link to your personal site, but no one has ever heard of you, then people won't click through. You'll send out a mass email, sending everyone your personal website without giving them any reason to click through. They're likely going to miss you.

If you give them a reason to click, then you have a better chance of getting them to convert. And if you give them a reason to convert, then you're on your way to being a real success. Once you have someone's email address, you have full permission to contact them. If you don't have permission, it's spam. There's nothing that tells the recipient you're a real person, so make sure you include a photo of yourself or whatever your profile is. **You don't always need to send your emails on behalf of the entire company!**

Also, keep it simple! To get the best results, avoid using your entire profile. You can put the profile link in the footer, or include it in the header of your email, so that they're aware you're a real person, and you're interested in them. When they click on the link in your email, this gives them a reason to know you. They're familiar with you, but they don't know you personally. So they're not going to guess. They're going to trust you if the demand is there and you package it right. If you make a compelling message and you do follow up, you can convert more subscribers. Always remember why your clients are interacting with you. For example, if you're a music store, you could include images that capture your reader's imagination!

Use a lot of personalization. Include information about your child's school, your wife's birthday, or whatever other details you can think of. Use all of your profile and include a lot of personalization.

Make sure that the click through is short and sweet. You want the person to feel compelled to go to your website. And, you want them to do so fast. After you've offered them the incentive, you don't want them to have to spend a lot of time figuring out how to get to your website. Don't ask them too many questions. Don't have them clicking on a link four times before you get your incentive.

Include a call to action in the email. All of your links should lead them to your landing page. This landing page should have a short and simple call to action. "Click here to learn more" is not going to cut it. You need to give them something more compelling than that.

So, using the above rules should help you get a lot more clicks in your email marketing campaign, and make more sales.

10. Email Marketing - The Groundwork

One of the biggest things that can kill your traditional marketing campaigns in the majority of cases is a lack of enthusiasm and inspiration. An email can't write and send itself unless directed to do so. But there's a catch!

In email marketing, you will often find that this is not the case. **Smarts outweigh hussle in the email game, especially with advanced tools on your side like autoresponders and sequences.** You have to be able to analyze your email marketing strategy to identify mistakes and make changes. There is a plethora of information and training on how to run a successful campaign on the web. The key to any email marketing campaign is to provide a compelling reason to open the email. If you fail to provide a reason why someone should open your email, chances are you have lost them forever.

But before we go on to look at what constitutes a compelling reason, we must first talk about subject lines. One of the most important elements of your subject line is the length of it. Your subject line should be no longer than 65 characters. It is imperative that you keep it under 65 characters so that it doesn't become a spam - even though many email programs can read it. Your subject line needs to **speak to the reader directly** so that it is not lost in the body of the email. This is a very important distinction and is not easily learned or practiced.

As you know, most spam filters are programmed to look for certain patterns of characters in an email subject line. Spammers have been creating spam subject lines that are intentionally misspelled and that use punctuation that is not standard. They also use misspelled subject lines and they use capital letters as opposed to lower case. Or use zero instead of letter "o."The point is, this can be a red flag for the spam filters and can get you filtered out of the server. To make sure this does not happen, stick to using the standard characters such as punctuation, hyphens and periods.

Here are some examples:

F.ree
LImITeD tIm.E OfFeR
$ave
0ffer

Next, the length of your subject line should be about 65 characters: not too short but also not too long. If you have to choose between short and long, choose short. You should keep them roughly even so that the emails are easy to scan and easy to read and familiar to the reader. The subject should be the first thing the reader notices so that they can recognize your email, open your email, and read it. You can also put some more descriptive text in the email. But do not use too much information. Don't overwhelm your reader with too much information. You want to be able to keep them interested with your email without taking up loads of their time. Let the bulk of the reading happen on your website or landing page, which could also help prime the reader for a potential sale or sign-up.

Another key aspect of your subject lines is that they should be personalized with the reader's name. So that they are more personal and warm. You can do this with the use of symbols which are a great way to accomplish this. They are the most personalized tool that has ever existed in marketing. But they should be used with care. Use them sparingly and don't do it so often that the recipient gets confused and thinks that your emails are spam. You want them to think that your emails are interesting and unique so that they will be driven to click on your links.

Once you have a compelling email subject line and a length that will get you through the filters, you now must have a compelling subject line and email body to get them to open your email, read it, and TAKE ACTION! The email body should be a sales pitch or an ad for your product, unless it serves a different function like branding, update, informative text, customer service, or special offer. In the end, prodive an option for your readers to escalate so that they can go to your link. But try to avoid spammy phrases and words because they can annoy your customers. Use phrases that are helpful and interesting to your customers. And lastly, you can use double opt-in. Don't make your subscriber make an effort to subscribe. The fact that they have to enter their email address and name at least 7 times makes them feel as if you're bothering them.

The most important aspect of having an email marketing campaign that is successful is the relationship that your customers have with you. If they have a good relationship with you, then they are likely to come back and purchase from you again. This is what we want, so don't put all your eggs in one basket. Email marketing should be a continuous process so that you get repeat sales from your campaigns.

Groundwork Case Study:

We did a case study!

From all the people who visited our website with a highly marketed sign-up form, around 12% subscribed or opted in! When you have a 100% opt-in list, I would expect to see something like 2 sales from every 300 emails, which would give you around 50 sales with 7,500 emails. This is in the first week of emailing. Of course, by this time, your list should be bigger. That doesn't mean you should stop sending out emails. I would not recommend you sending out more than 4 emails a week. There is simply too much activity in the email market today, and not enough buyers to soak up the activity.

You can make your emails more personal. People are more often more willing to hear your pitch if you address them by name in the subject line, and in the body of the email. That means the subject line and body of the email are your two bread and butter. Your bread and butter is what sells you and your email. The reason why you have a good email pitch is because it worked. You addressed the prospect in the subject line, you seasoned your offer in the body, you redirected them to a landing page or funnel and showed them why they should buy from you.

You can get people to take the next step by making them feel like a genius. Make the offer interesting. If you address them personally, by name in the subject line, you can make them feel special. Add a picture and make them feel like they are a genius for opening the email. People like being addressed personally. In the body of the email, you should address them again, just like in the subject line, but in a different way.

Instead of asking them to buy, you ask them to click on "how to use it." Make them feel like they are smarter with your product than their peers. Your bread and butter is your ability to produce real AND perceived value. So if your bread and butter is selling, and that's all you are trying to do, then you need to add some other marketing strategies like advertising or an affiliate program. Add any form of marketing to your email pitch, and you can get a higher response.

11. Unique and Valuable Email Marketing Campaigns

To achieve the optimum results from your email marketing, it is important to focus on a few guidelines while creating your messages.

1. Use the right words to convey the right message. In email marketing, you are selling a service, not a product. So avoid using words like Free, Sale, Give Away, Guarantee that usually denote a sales message.

2. Short, get to the point and include alternative links. Email marketing is all about content not flashy graphics or graphics with high-resolution images. Think about customer needs, not marketing skills. If you want to attract customers to open your emails, make sure that they would find your content very useful and worthwhile reading. Provide a link to your web page to allow them to get to know more about your service.

3. Personalize your emails. Don't be overly formal or speak in a corporate style. Speak to your audience in the same way you would to a friend. If you have a problem that you want to share with your audience, use an email instead of regular mail. It gives you the opportunity to address the problem personally, instead of referring to someone.

Don't put in the subject line "the secret of making $X", or "we couldn't have done it without you". While they may be great subject lines, you do not need to include them in every email that you send. Just let them be a part of some of your biggest marketing campaigns.

What makes a great email? How do you know it is a great email? You, as the recipient, can say "wow, this content is really valuable and worthwhile reading", not "wow, this content is great", not the boss, not the mother, not the child, not the relative, not the boss' cousin etc. You are worth it. Your value to your audience.

Don't go overboard with your graphics and flashy graphics. Leave it alone unless it is absolutely necessary and try to put in a link with the most basic graphics. Put the link in the middle of the email and use plain text.

When a great company sends out an email in the right way, you will definitely want to receive it. If your company sends a great email, people should definitely want to look at it. It's got the logo, it's got a catchy, fun, and memorable subject line. It has a great logo that has great text and design. It has compelling, great and unique content. It uses the full potential of your email and tells about an exciting and valuable success story that is worth looking at. It should not send you another email unless you look at it. You see, it has been worth it.

You have to find out what exactly people want to read in your newsletter and write to meet that need. The newsletter can either be a sales piece, which can result in orders, or it can be a marketing piece, which can lead to more subscribers and more orders. It is the time to evaluate what is appealing to your audience and incorporate the information that should bring you the greatest results. So, if you decide to write about discounts, what are the basic requirements in terms of the information you should include in the newsletter.

The first thing to include in your newsletter is content. Here are some questions you should ask yourself to find out what people would like to know about, or what are the questions they would like to have answered in your newsletter. What are the biggest issues in the industry? How can you solve that issue? What is the most important thing that you should address in your newsletter?

Now you also need to know what the focus of your newsletter should be on. For instance, if you decide to focus on product discounts, then write about the top 10 best selling products, or the top 3 best selling products. For affiliate marketers, write about the top 3 best selling programs.

Finally, you also need to decide the length of your newsletter. There are two common approaches to writing your newsletter. The first one is the traditional newsletter. It is the newsletter that contains a full topic, which is a topic that always includes all the essential information about the topic. The second approach is a review piece or summary. In this type of approach, your newsletter will usually contain just the first few paragraphs about the topic and then include the rest in the summary section. The length of your newsletter has to be long enough to be informative, but short enough not to be too boring.

Once you know how to write an email newsletter, you now have some challenges ahead. The first challenge is to find out what your audience wants to read. I suggest you do a survey to your subscribers. Find out what they want to read and then write your email newsletter on the topics that these people want to read. The results from your survey can give you good ideas on what products you should promote. The second challenge is to find someone who wants to give you their time on your newsletter.

To find someone who wants to give you their time on your newsletter, send out an email to them and offer them that. You can either use the paid method or the invited method of finding people who want to give you their time. The third challenge is also to write and to write content that is very informative and very helpful. It is very important to write something that is educational, but not so much that it becomes boring.

The fourth challenge is to also give something away in your email newsletter. You can give away an eBook or a trial version of a software or a video. This can help the recipients pass the time.

The fifth challenge is to include people's names in the content. In order for the email newsletter to be more effective, the names of people are necessary included. You can write the names of people in the body of the email or you can include the names in the subject line. This can help the recipients recognize their names.

The sixth challenge is to have a good layout. It is very important to make the content easy to read. The newsletter should also be in a good layout so that the recipients can get the most out of it. You can use templates to make it easy. Alternatively, try to create a very flashy email with plenty of HTML and see how you do. Sometimes, a traditional email with just a hint of flash is the best way to go.

The seventh challenge is to also make the content personal. To make it personal, use the recipients' name twice and add another element highly relevant to them like location or occupation. The eighth challenge is to make sure that the email newsletter includes a "limited time offer" type of thing. The ninth challenge is to try to have a good landing page so that the recipient does not need to be familiarized with the email newsletter before they complete the survey.

The tenth challenge is to also have a feedback page so that the respondents can give you their opinions. The feedback page can be used to ask the respondents what they want. It can also be used to help you decide on the direction you want to take. Then, if you want, try adding a how-to video in your email!

12. Email Marketing: Use This Powerful Tool

When you consider the fact that email marketing is one of the most powerful marketing tools you can use for your business, you can find that your business can gain a lot of revenue, and also save a lot of time. Therefore, you should use email marketing to enhance the efficiency of your business. When you start to use email marketing to send out your communications, you should make sure that you have a good grasp of this powerful tool, otherwise you can find that your business is not benefiting from this marketing strategy. Email marketing is both a CRM system and a sales pipeline, which makes it so unique.

Some of the most successful marketers online today have around 500,000 subscribers to their lists and maintain them with only a couple of servers. That is a huge difference to what you might have seen on the web a few years ago. You can use the same principle to build your own list, however the internet requires you to have a good quality mailing list to be successful. It is all about relevance. If you can mail your list frequently, then you are more likely to get a good response. If you cannot, then you are better off starting a new list and making your email marketing campaign work with a new list.

The best part about email marketing is the ability to market your product or service using only one email and have your marketing funnel work for you. As a result, it is also easy to generate a high level of return on investment from a single mailing campaign.

- Targeted list : You can target your email campaigns for the best response by segmenting your list. What this means is that you can identify those who have the highest response to your particular product or service. Then by mailing a particular piece of information to your list, you can see better results. The downside to this is that you can lose those that do not respond to your initial effort. I know I would definitely start over and begin a new campaign if I was creating an email marketing campaign.

- Free information : You have to offer your visitors something for free to get them to sign up to your list. It could be a report, newsletter, or videos. The best way to give away free information is to have your opt-in form or squeeze page above the fold of the page. This way your visitors should not be able to leave the page or scroll down without signing up.

- The use of your email lists : You can use your existing lists as an email marketing campaign. The best way to do this is to send your mailings out with your own personalised content. This way, your subscribers can know who is sending them emails.

- Pay per click : You can pay per click by including links within your email which can get your traffic to your site.

The key to successful email marketing is to provide information in your email that is useful to the subscriber and have your sales funnel work for you. Remember, this is your marketing funnel. You want to get them to the point where they are ready to sign up.

If your email marketing campaign does not work, you can easily start over with a new campaign. You can get a new email marketing system set up quickly. After you set up your system, you can track who is opening your emails and click-throughs. Your campaign should provide feedback on how well it is working for you.

This feedback can help you refine your marketing funnel and improve your website. And remember that just because you can track these statistics does not mean you should. It can give you good information but not good action.

13. How to Make Money With a Newsletter

You may have spent a great deal of time creating an informative email newsletter. It has an attractive layout that catches your readers' attention. However, what happens to all those pictures and text that would normally go with an email newsletter? How will you make money from a newsletter?

If you're like most Internet marketers, you'd have your subscribers opt in. That means they agree to receive your newsletters. You get the address of their email address, and then you use what is called an autoresponder to send them your newsletter.

The great thing about an auto responder is that it automatically sends the newsletters out to everyone who opts in to the list. In fact, auto responders are a fantastic way to make money from email lists.

First, all you have to do is send a newsletter to your mailing list, and the autoresponder handles the rest. You don't have to do anything but send it out. What you want to do is set it up so that when someone opts into your list, they get the newsletter automatically. For example, if you had a list of 30,000 contacts, and 5,000 of those subscribe, you send a newsletter out to 5,000 people on the same day. As soon as 5,000 people get it, you start making money from your list.

Of course, what you do after you start making money from your email list is to send out other newsletters to other parts of your email list. That is what is called cross selling. All you have to do is create another email, and start sending it out to other parts of your email or contact list. You would not stop sending out to the same people even after you started making money from your email list. What you want to do is to create another email, and then create another email, and another email, etc. etc.

It's a simple process, and once you do it once, you should be good to go. Just remember that it takes practice to build up a good relationship with your list. It's also important to create compelling newsletters to your subscribers. Your newsletter should be informative, and it should always have some type of content.

You should be able to find lots of information on how to build a successful business online. You can find lots of helpful tips and tricks and you should be able to build a successful business online. It's actually a very easy process. You should be able to be good to go and be profitable from your list any time you want. You should be able to set it up in no time. You should be able to make money from your email list any time you want. That's the advanced art of email marketing. Your primed subscriber's list is your cash cow!

I hope that you find this article helpful. Remember that it takes practice to build up a relationship with your list. It's actually a very easy process that you can do whenever you want, given the necessary conditions are met.

Increasing Delivery Rates

As an internet marketer, you will most likely be sending and receiving emails in bulk at least once or twice a day. The more you send and receive in email, the more your emails can become indistinguishable from the rest. So if you're going to get your emails opened, you need to get your readers to remember your brand name. But if your email campaign is not making an impact on your prospects, the first thing you must focus on is the quality of your email.

First of all, writing a subject line is similar to composing poetry. One of the keys to writing a captivating email subject is to use a few effective words in your subject line. This is where you use words that your prospects can identify with. Words like Free, Offer, Reasons, Benefits and More.

In the main body of your email body, you want to highlight the main benefit of your offer and tell them about the action you want them to take. These are just some of the actions you can take. You may have to work on the message, as it is the message that will lead your prospects to the landing page, and that landing page will be your final destination. You should be able to track the conversion rate in your email marketing campaign. There are a few tools that can help you to track these things out.

There are many tools that can help you with your campaign and tracking these things out, with tools, you can have the chance to find out how many times your emails were opened. From the tracking, you should be able to know the conversion rate in your campaign. It is important that you know that tracking the things out can give you the best chances of your emails being opened.

- Tracking your emails can give you detailed information on which links in the email went to which page.

- Tracking your emails can help you to improve the subject line of your email, and the opening rate of your emails. This can help you to improve the subject line of the next email.

- In email marketing, one of the most valuable things to offer your prospects is a video. The video should be short. It should explain the benefits of the product you are selling in short phrases and then a call to action is what your prospects should click. If you can add the call to action to the beginning of your video, you can improve your click through rate.

- When your prospect clicks on the link in your video, it is a good idea to offer them free advice, tips or something you have discovered. This is a good way to improve your click through rate.

- If you are selling a webinar, offer them a transcript of the webinar. The transcript should include the questions that were asked in the live broadcast. If you did not have an audio or video feed in your webinar, you can improve your click through rate.

- When your prospects are in the process of clicking on your links, they should see a box that they should enter their name and email address. This is a good idea to improve your opt-in rate and be able to get additional information such as country and state.

- Try to create eye-catching paragraphs with an interesting subject line. You should be able to use your bullet points and short sentences.

- For your email marketing campaign, it is a good idea to include a link to a survey. This is a good way to improve the speed and quality of your email delivery.

14. Five Things to Consider in Email Marketing

Email marketing is one of the better ways of communicating with potential customers. It should be kept in mind that your email campaign should be crafted in such a way that it not only gives information on products and services but also builds trust.

This article will focus on how to build trust in your email list which can go a long way in ensuring a profitable email campaign.

1. Avoid using the word FREE when you can use the word Discount. This is a very important rule that every marketer should remember. If you are to create a discount marketing campaign then you can mention how your products are discounted to the point that the product is only available on your website. But when you mention the word FREE then it can look suspicious to the customer.

2. Use the customer's name in the email. If you want to build a trusting relationship with the customer then you must use their name in the email. Customers do trust others who use their name in the email so try and use it sparingly in your email campaign.

3. Make sure your customers are happy with your products and services. Try and find out what they like and what they don't like. If you find out what they don't like then you can change it to suit them better. If you find out what they like then you can make the product even better for them.

4. Try and ask for some feedback on the products or services. If you are asking for feedback on products then make sure you mention how your product can really benefit them.

5. The email campaign is only as good as the database you have so try and obtain feedback from the subscribers on your mailing list. If the customers are happy with the products or services then it can be easier for you to make a sale to them.

The success of your email campaign relies on how well your list of subscribers and your email campaign plays to your customer's deepest desires and tendencies. So try to implement these and really get to understand the mentality of your customers to be successful.

15. Keep Your Emails Short, Direct and to the Point

Many people struggle with getting their marketing messages delivered to their customers, so this article is written for those people. In this article I'm going to describe a few of the things you can do to improve the delivery of your emails and other marketing messages. The most important thing you should do is start using a good auto responder right from the beginning.

Once you have started using a good autoresponder you should try to make it your business partner. This can make you more profitable because you'll be able to contact people whenever you want.

One thing you should always do is try to have a good subject line for your email. This is the first thing anyone sees when they open up their email account and your subject line can be a big factor in whether or not they can read the rest of your email.

Another thing that you should do is create a good email template. If you use a lot of graphics and HTML code then you might have a tough time getting past the spam filters. So try to keep your emails as simple as possible. If you're using HTML and graphics then you should probably create a plain text template or at least an email template that can make it past the spam filters. This way anyone who sees your email should know it's a marketing email and won't be surprised when they see a lot of other emails in their inbox.

Another thing you should keep in mind is that spam filters may be looking at the content of your email and your subject line. If you write a subject line that promises something and then add an explicit graphic or warning then this can show up in spam filters as well. So keep your subject lines limited to a plain text. That way it will likely be harder for spam filters to catch everything.

Finally, if you have a lot of pictures or graphics in your emails, then the spam filters could see this as a sign of spam and they could put your email in the spam folder. So keep your emails short and concise. Think of the spam filters as the school yard bullies. They'll be a lot more likely to submit your email to the spam folder if you keep your emails concise. You want them to submit your email, but it should be a last resort.

The truth of the matter is that getting the email past the spam filters is more of a science than it is an art. The best advice I can give you is to keep your emails short, direct and to the point. If you do this then the spam filters can be less likely to see it as spam. Then you should also create email templates for when you have a lot of graphics and other images. You never know when you might need them.

Your email list is your greatest asset and unfortunately many marketers fail to utilize it the right way. You need to focus on building a relationship with your list as opposed to just trying to get them to sign up for your list thinking that you can earn money off of them. If you truly want to create a long term sustainable business model you must focus on building a relationship with your list and offering value.

If you send promotional emails out every day expecting to get sales you are on the wrong track and not following the right track. The majority of people don't mind receiving promotions so long as the promotion is quality. The majority of people can no longer stay on your list if you continuously send out promo emails but do not provide any value. If you want to make more sales you need to provide value and by providing value you should see an increase in your sales. If you don't provide value you are just wasting your time and causing you to lose subscribers as well.

16. Are You Sending Emails to the Wrong People?

Email marketing has been around for many years, but with the increase of speed and ease of communication on the internet, it has become one of the most useful marketing tools available on the internet today. This form of direct marketing works by sending an email to a list of subscribers who have subscribed to it. This is an opportunity to talk with your customers, or interested customers.

There are many advantages to email marketing, here are three examples:

1) Email marketing provides a very quick way of talking to people. This can be a special promotion for your product, an announcement of a special event, etc. It's very easy to send an email, even for those that don't have access to a computer. It can be a very quick form of promotion and marketing in general.

2) Email marketing allows you to get an immediate response, this is helpful in the area of service and quality. It's much easier to get your product to people, to get people to take a particular action that you want them to take in the first place, or ask for information that you want them to look at. It's much easier to get people to view your special promotion or information. It can help with satisfaction.

3) This form of marketing allows you to stay in contact with your customers and subscribers on a regular basis. This is a good way to develop and maintain a relationship with your customers. This is a good way to keep your current customers informed about new developments in your products and services.

Now let's look at some disadvantages. It's important to consider some of the disadvantages of this marketing method when you're getting started, because there are some disadvantages that you can run into.

When you're getting started, you need to know your numbers. If you're doing a mass mailing to a large list, you will need to use a mailing list software program that can give you accurate data for how many emails were sent, how many recipients opened the email, and how many were clicked through.

If you're sending emails to a large list, you should also know how many recipients opened your email, how many recipients click through, and how many opened your email in a particular week.

If you're doing a promotional email, you should know the links that were used. For example, if your email is a promotional email, you should know if someone clicked on the button to return to your website.

If you're using an email marketing software program, you should also know how many recipients have opened your email, how many recipients have clicked on your links, and how many have unsubscribed from your mailing list.

When You're Getting Started

- If you're sending a promotional email, you should also know how many recipients are opening your email, how many recipients are clicking on your links, and how many recipients are unsubscribing from your mailing list
- Segment your list by income, age, location, industry, purchasing habits, and more until you discover the perfect way to segment your list!
- Follow the best-practices especially when it comes to email etiquette and laws
- Keep it interesting but short
- Set up regular outflows of emails by using automators and sequences
- Drive traffic to a funnel or landing page
- Persuade users to share your content (ie newsletters) on social media!
- Integrate email marketing with other marketing channels like social media and phone
- Make your emails personal and intriguing
- Avoid spammy language and don't send unsolicited emails
- Try adding some HTML, JavaScript, and flash when appropriate but don't overdo
- Keep your subject lines brief, around the 65 character marker
- Dissect your analytics to find new opportunities for improvement
- Don't be afraid to implement trial and error

17. Email Marketing Campaigns: Your Account Manager

To begin with, email marketing as a whole has become a complex affair. This is because it must be used as a means to build relationships both internally within organisations and externally with customers.

As an internal means, how many individuals and how many organisations are you working with when you initiate an email marketing campaign?

Initiating an email marketing campaign is easier to do when there are already relationships forming between internal people and your organisation. For example, your sales people and your procurement people work together for a particular product or service.

Your web designer works together with your account manager for a particular service. Everyone within your organisation is familiar with the type of email service they use. The quality of the service they are using and the level of service they provide is very high. It's therefore much easier to have an email marketing campaign initiated through their channels, rather than yours. It's as simple as that.

However, it's also very common to initiate an email marketing campaign from your organisation's website if you've utilised the service of a web designer. This is because it's quite an unusual site and you can use the service of someone familiar with the service you utilised.

If you're using an external service to initiate an email marketing campaign then the process is very different. You don't get a level of build-up with your account manager, sales person or web designer. You just send the email out and it's dealt with in one of your normal channels. So you can initiate an email marketing campaign from your main website account, from your main business account or from your sales account.

These different processes mean that you need to learn a bit of specific technical language. It's important to understand the difference between who you're communicating with and how you're communicating with them. Also, the technical term for the process is "list building". In technical terms, email marketing is a process. And processes are more efficient than "lists".

Email marketing requires a bit of know-how and technical know-how. If you don't have these then your campaigns may be ineffective. The technical know-how, in relation to email marketing, is about utilising an "autoresponder". It's important to understand what an "autoresponder" is. It's part of an automation programme that allows you to send emails out automatically. This is important because not all organisations utilise an autoresponder. Your autoresponder must be able to take over the function of the account manager, sales person or web designer.

If your main account manager is not familiar with the autoresponder then you need to ensure they get to learn about it as part of their role. As part of their role you also need to ensure they are familiar with the way emails are managed, the controls that are available and the technical language you need to use.

The technical language about email marketing involves the use of "CTR". It also involves a control that is called a "senders list". As part of their role your main account manager will probably need to send emails out to the subscribers on their list in order to gather new subscribers as well as monitoring the response from them.

You will probably find that not all of your subscribers are going to respond. You should be able to communicate this to your account manager so that they can set up a different campaign for those subscribers.

Also, it's important to be able to monitor how many people are opening your emails. As well as the frequency that you send out your emails you also need to be able to track the click through rate. You will probably need to be able to monitor this to make sure it increases over time.

These are just some of the elements of an email marketing campaign. There are of course many other, more technical but easier elements such as which email systems you should use, who you should send it to, the design which should be in HTML or text and how many times the email should be displayed. It's important that they all are familiar with these important details in order for your email marketing campaign to be successful.

18. Email Marketing - The Making of a Marketing Campaign

Have you ever received an email that reads: "I have received your name and email address from a trusted source. They should be contacting you within the next 24 hours to confirm your order"? Well, that doesn't happen. And if it did, I'd certainly be disappointed. Why? If I can't trust one stranger, why do you think I would trust two strangers?

The answer is this: email marketing's purpose is to form relationships with the people on your email list. The people who have kindly signed up to receive information from you. As an internet marketer, your job is to build a relationship with them, to convince them that you're someone they can trust. When you rely on them completely, however, you're also relying on them not eating you up from the inside out. In other words, you need to give them plenty of opportunities to tell you off if they feel you're taking advantage of them. Avoid using phrases like "trust me" or "let me be frank" or "let me be honest." If someone says "let me be honest…" it implies that they think honesty applies to one moment but not another.

I receive plenty of emails from marketers who would dearly love to have my email address, so why bother opening them? It's one of the many reasons I don't open emails from marketers. The only reason I open them, other than the trust factor, is because they have something for me to look at, some interesting snippets of information that should interest me. Or else, I would simply delete them. Which begs the question, "Why do I open them?" It's a question I have asked myself numerous times.

Well, honestly, I do it for the curiosity factor. I open them simply because I don't want to lose that encounter. I was curious enough to open. I want to see what they have to offer. I'm more likely to open them if I know I'm going to get an informative piece of information. I'm more likely to open them again in a fortnight's time if I'm interested in what's contained within. If I'm curious, I'll open them every day until I have had my fill. If I'm bored, I'll delete them straight away. So, there you go. Another juicy reason why you should make the effort to get your email opened. It might not be as quick as Facebook or Twitter, but it will probably more than pay for itself in the long run.

E-mail has revolutionized the way that we communicate with each other and with our business partners. It is much easier to communicate in writing and online campaigns are far less labor intensive than those that occur in person.

E-mail is a convenient way to communicate with your followers. It is also a popular channel for spammers to use. A lot of people are careful about opening messages that arrive in their email inboxes. Your message has to stand out in the crowded field that may contain a dozen other messages that have been generated by various marketing efforts and are waiting to be opened.

What happens when people open messages in their email?

Sometimes it may contain useful and relevant information while sometimes it may contain a barrage of promotions and other times it may contain nothing. It is important to know the difference so that you can avoid the probability of being classified as a spammer and also get your message read by your followers.

When you are communicating via email, make sure that you deliver the message and your prospects feel that you have not forgotten them.

You have a choice of two methods of doing this.

1. You can send repeated emails containing the same message. You can set up a series of emails to build up to the moment when they might feel as though they have received useful communication, then you can make them click on a link.

2. You can create a different message which builds up until a moment that they might feel as though they have understood your message and then delivered your offer. This is where the click on a link comes from. You can set up a separate email to be delivered after a certain period of time and you can create a link to go to your separate website. It

is important to create a split second decision in your followers so that you can develop a marketing campaign that is a success. By doing this you are building up a business that could last for years.

An email campaign aims at providing new information about a particular product to customers who have signed up for it on the internet. Direct marketing has become a new age form of marketing due to its fast track success in acquiring new customers. When doing email marketing, online marketers are required to be very smart about what they send to customers.

If you have not done this before, an email is sent to a customer and after that customer signs up and subscribes to your email list. A direct email can be sent to a specific customer but a welcome email. can be sent to the customer who subscribed to your email list. If this customer becomes a loyal customer and subscribes to your email list in future, this email can become a welcome letter.

Most marketers are using HTML based email marketing. They feel that they are sending the HTML message in the email. In most cases they are not. Here's an example. The email message is the message in the message storehouse. That message contains the graphic and text content which can be shown on the e-mail message. Those graphics and text content are sent by a server. The browser who goes to the website has to download those graphic and text content. If the customer opens the email, a "back" button is provided by the company which can take the customer to the previous page. Those graphic and text content would be loaded from the message storehouse and can be sent as an attachment from that specific attachment. All those facts allow marketers to test different graphics and text content for their response.

There is a test company can use which shows them how to send different graphics and text content to the customer. There is a specific text message that is sent. The customer is asked to open the message. The particular text message was chosen based on the particular customer and the particular graphic had to be loaded for the specific customer. The particular customers are interested in the particular graphic and text content. The particular email is sent to the particular customer and they subscribed.

If the graphic and text content is not loaded, then the specific email cannot be opened. If you can not open the particular graphic and text content in the first email sent, then there is no way to continue the relationship between the company and the specific customer.

If you have a particular product which is a gift, a limited offer for your customer is only sent once. The customers are not given a second chance to order the product. If you have a lot of products, then you may send the product to different email addresses. The product is available on several sites which are part of the particular customer group.

19. Discover The Secrets Of Email Marketing

In order to establish a strong relationship with your prospects, an effective email marketing campaign is a vital component of your marketing campaign strategy. After all, the recipients of your marketing emails can be the future customers of your products and services. And you want them to purchase your products and services when they're ready to make a purchase. In order to do that, you must maintain a strong relationship with these prospective customers, otherwise why are you doing marketing?

Effective email marketing is an important task that does not come easy. If you are new to the internet marketing game, then perhaps this is a foreign concept to you. What is email marketing? Essentially, it is sending an email to a targeted group of people who have shown an interest in receiving that specific marketing email. This is done through an auto-responder service. Now what is an auto-responder service? Basically, it is a software service that allows marketers to easily send automatic emails to targeted people on an opt-in basis. In simple terms, it is an auto-responder service that allows you to send an email to every person who has shown an interest in receiving marketing emails.

Now that you understand the basics, let us take a look at some specific tips you should follow to make your email marketing campaign successful and effective.

1. Set up your email lists - you can either organize your lists by category or by individual prospects, but not both. This is important so that your emails should be relevant to the recipients.

2. Create attractive subject lines - the subject lines of your emails should be clear, relevant and should touch your audience's emotions in some way. This could make them open your emails.

3. Choose the best time to send your email - this may depend on the kind of business you are running. Some businesses thrive during the work week, while others do best

during the weekends. You might need to determine the best time for your campaign to be effective.

4. Don't sell too much - Your email marketing should be helpful without over selling your products or services. Do this by sharing information that will help your prospects to understand your product and why they should buy it.

5. Provide a call to action - remember that you are selling products or services, not a product or service. The call to action is the link they need to click on in your email to buy your products. This link should be helpful and educational so that the prospect gets what they are looking for.

6. Track your campaign - you may need to track and analyze your campaign so that you can find out what works best. You can do this by looking at click through rates (CTR), open rates (RO), opt-out rates (OU) and unsubscribe rates (UR). These can tell you which ones worked the best.

These are the basics of email marketing. I encourage you to learn more about this form of marketing and apply these basic techniques in your business. The internet is a great place to learn more about anything that you want to learn more about.

20. Mastering Email Marketing

Email is fast becoming a regular source of communication in the modern world, more popular even than postal mail. But like anything else, it has its own good points and also its own faults, which are just waiting to be exploited. Here are a few ways to master email marketing:

1. Create a database of email addresses. Do not lose them! If you are building a list from scratch, you need to start by creating a database of email addresses that you can use as your 'starting point'. Keep it updated regularly and constantly. If something happens to that database, you have lost a potential source of customers for your business.

2. Keep the database current. You need to use every opportunity to add new addresses to the list. Make it a habit of keeping a list of all addresses on your site. Also try to collect every mention of your business in emails and correspondence, wherever it may appear.

3. Be consistent. Your message must be delivered consistently. If you send email messages too frequently (more than twice a week) they can start to feel like spam. On the other hand, if you don't send email messages at all they can seem like a total waste of time.

4. Don't overdo it. Don't send too many emails, at the same time or to the same person.

It is important to note that marketing by email has its own set of rules which are quite different from the rules of traditional marketing, where you make offers one after the other. In email marketing you have to be very careful, not to create the impression that you are spamming and not to create the impression that you don't care about the outcome of your marketing campaigns. It is not enough to send one email to someone, you need to send three, or four, or five. Each email should have information in it that would not be possible if you didn't send the email.

To master email marketing, it is important to recognize that 'the game' is much different from the game of traditional marketing. Be ready to adapt to the rules and understand how to work within them. Be ready to adjust your marketing techniques to keep your customers satisfied and interested in what you are offering.

The internet has a number of uses. For example, the World Wide Web is used for a number of purposes, one of which is email. It is the standard way of sending information around the globe.

An email service provider is one that can provide the email services that you can use. For example, if you want to send photos to someone in Australia then you may use an email service provider in Australia. Then they send them on. The company that you will hire will cater to the email service provider that will carry out all of these functions.

The company should handle the whole process for you, including autoresponders and automation sequences. It is cheaper and it can get you back to doing the important things that you want to be doing which is messaging, messaging, messaging. Now I want to talk to you about sending the emails in the first place.

If you can think like a marketer, then you should be able to make email marketing work for you. It is a process that you can use in your marketing all the time. When you are sending your emails, you need to use good subject lines because they could help you get a better open rate.

The point of an email is to provide your reader with the information that you want them to have. Your email should provide them with more information than you expected them to need.

Your email should always provide value for money and that is your objective. This means that the value that you provide your reader should always be greater than the cost. You need to always look to the other person's advantage and always focus on the customer's benefit.

Sending emails is the easiest task because all you have to do is think like a marketer and send your emails out that you want to get to the person that you want to get to. This is the point where you become a marketer.

21. Why Companies Send Emails

Email marketing has become an essential component of marketing for many companies today. It has proven to be a successful means of acquiring customers for businesses. As email marketing has grown more, companies have tried various ways to use it and have utilized them to make their business grow. Some of the ways are outlined here.

1. Sending Emails to acquire new customers.

Companies send email to capture and retain new leads. They try to entice customers to purchase the products and services by offering a money back guarantee. They try to increase customer loyalty by offering customer discounts on subsequent orders and by providing fast delivery. They try to make new leads feel welcome and accepted by sending them welcome messages on their birthday. This is done to give them a special day in their calendar.

2. Sending Emails to maintain relationships with existing customers.

Companies send emails to make their existing customers feel appreciated by sending them thank you messages on their birthday. They also send occasional promotional emails to ensure the continuing patronage of their existing customer base. These are just some of the ways in which companies try to maintain and establish the level of relationship with their customer. They do this by offering different services and products on their website. They also offer support, consultation and other services on a consignment basis. They try to create a strong bond of customer loyalty by reminding customers of their purchase, the day of their purchase, and so on. This is done by offering value-based pricing.

When a person is online and browsing through the pages of a website the chances are that he is most likely to stop by the products page. But what is a product page? An email marketing website should give the users an insight on the products that the company is dealing with and also provide the users with the way for customers to contact the company for more information.

When the users go to the homepage of the company, then there should be an email opt-in page, which should be a well structured and attractive page, which should not be buried under a mountain of information. It should provide the users with the information about how they can request for more information or what should be their next step. This page should not make the users feel like they are pestered by a salesperson.

In the email marketing campaign, the email opt-in page is the first part where the company should present to the customers. If the page is not attractive then chances are that the visitors should not bother to opt-in. It should contain something in which the visitor should get impressed. This may include an attention grabbing headline, a few benefits, an FAQ and an opt-in form, which would be the first thing the users need to register for the emails.

If the visitors opt-in they are given some basic information about the company, how to use the product, the estimated cost of the product, what should be expected after they opt- in. After they opted in they should be given a confirmation email which they are asked to reply to. This is in case they intend to cancel the subscription. This is in order to avoid a spam complaint against the company.

It should be mentioned here that a company which is dealing with the online business industry should provide these things as they are important in order to ease the concerns of the visitors. The customers who opt in, should be given the right support, which means they are not scammed into thinking that the company has little interest in them. This is because a person who is interested in his product has signed up in order to find out the costumer's cost and the future of his product. It is also in order to offer the subscriber some information, which is in line with the needs of the customer.

On the other hand, when a user opts out he should be given some information about his request. This is in order to ease his concern and because of which the company can follow-up his inquiry.

These are just a few ways companies use email marketing. However, these are only some of the ways. They try to find new ways to use this popular marketing tool in their business. They do this by doing market research and gathering knowledge on the customers' preferences to give them the best possible email marketing solution for their business. The next article will delve into how they create attractive and professional email campaigns.

Stay tuned. We will get into how they create attractive and professional email campaigns.

22. The Secret to Email Marketing Success: Giving!

Email marketing is an extremely effective form of marketing, when executed properly. In fact, it is a great way to increase your customer base and your sales while offering the kind of repeat customer relations that will likely make you untraceable.

One thing to remember with email marketing, is that you need to approach it with the same urgency you would your direct mail marketing. This means that you need to treat your email marketing as if it were a direct mail piece. This could ensure that you get the results you are looking for.

Let's take a look at how one might approach this through email marketing. One can send them an email saying something like, "Want to save 20% off?" This could definitely get your reader's attention, and even get them to click on your link, so the results are obvious.

Another way is to offer a free gift, then a discount, then a free gift. These two links can get you the leads that are necessary for your business to grow. You could even offer a discount, and then a free gift for reading your newsletter.

Another tactic to consider is the fact that, once your reader trusts you, you have the opportunity to give them something in return. You should not be afraid of trying this, because it can only boost your results. Give them a good product or service, and then send them a free gift. If the gift is good, and if the service is good, then the results might be even better, if you continue to send the reader good information.

As you can see, email marketing has become a great way to make it in business, but there is more to it than meets the eye. There is a science to it, and you must learn about this science to become a master email marketer.

If you want to introduce your mailing list to a new product or service, give a sample of it as a free gift! If your service is worth it, many customers who appreciate your free gift may surely be interested. The key is to give without fearing about getting back in return. The harvest comes naturally after the seeds have been planted. As an email marketer, your job is to plant as many positive seeds in your future customer's minds as you can -- and do it in a chilled manner.

One of the many benefits of an email marketing campaign is that your target market is not necessarily confined to just your target audience. In fact, by targeting your audience you narrow your target market dramatically. It is much easier to attract new prospects when your focus is on their problems. If you focus on their comfort and convenience then they may not be interested in your product or service that much. In order to ensure that you get an optimal return on your investment to the extent that you can, you should focus on creating value for your target market. If they feel that your service or product is valuable to them then you have a good chance of getting a very high amount of return on investment.

It is always very important to make sure that your email marketing campaign is not viewed as spam. One of the methods to achieve this is with SPAM filters. When your email arrives in the inbox of your target audience they must evaluate whether or not it is spam. SPAM filters are software programs that look at each and every email that arrives in their inbox. If it passes the test of either of these filters you may be blocked by the filter. By having SPAM filters you lose out on an opportunity to get your message to your market.

You can still get your message out there if you use an email marketing campaign. There are many benefits of using an email marketing campaign. It allows you to instantly reach a wide area of people. It also allows for great opportunities to give your client a taste of your product. By giving them a taste of your product, they might then be interested in your product and what it can do for them.

When you first begin using an email marketing campaign you may learn a lot about your audience. For instance if your target market is young and tech savvy then you can definitely want to include a tech coupon in your email. These types of coupons allow you to give your client a taste of your product, which could then encourage them to go to your site to learn more. As they learn more, they could then be even more intrigued by the product and you have a high chance of getting a high return on your investment.

One of the best things about using an email marketing campaign is that it allows you to reach your target market in no time. By using an email marketing campaign you do not have to wait for several weeks to months for your campaign to reach your audience. It takes seconds for you to send your campaign. This is a great way to get your message out there to the world. Also it allows you to learn your target market's preferences and the types of promotions that they are most interested in. This allows you to develop future promotions based on these preferences. This allows you to quickly market your product in the future.

When you begin using an email marketing campaign, you might realize it's a great way to get your message out there quickly. It also allows you to learn from your email marketing campaigns. As you develop future email marketing campaigns you might be able to learn more about your market, and create future campaigns based on their interests. Using an email marketing campaign helps you quickly market your product.

23. Email Marketing - Tips on Writing an Email That Gets Opened

There is a problem with email marketing that your business is likely to experience. While it may be tempting to spend as much time as possible with the prospect, if you do not take the time to develop a relationship, the odds are they can unsubscribe from your emails. In addition, you will likely be accused of spamming them, because they signed up for your service, but you ended up emailing them hundreds of emails. They could not only accuse you of spamming, they could ask to be removed from your mailing list, resulting in potential harm to your business

Tip #1 - Treat each email like a personal message. When you are developing a relationship with your email list members, it is important to take things very seriously. Don't talk to them in terms of "Business Email". Don't talk in terms of "Business Email Marketing". Instead use the business email form of address and talk to them like you are talking to a friend or a colleague. People love this approach, because they know you are not trying to steal their business or anything.

Tip #2 - Keep it short and sweet. If you really need to give them a lot of information in your email, try to make sure that you limit it to a reasonable number of points. If you need to give them a lot of information, try to go on "one by one" as much as possible. And if you don't have the time to make it too detailed, try to make it as brief as possible.

Tip #3 - Make sure you are writing for them, rather than for yourself. Always be aware that your audience is reading what you are writing for them. If you are writing to your list about "business email", make sure you are talking to them about your own business. That is why it is important that you create a relationship with them and treat them as fellow business people.

4. Make sure your emails are memorable. You need to make sure your emails are memorable. It takes a certain kind of personality to run an email marketing campaign. You need to be able to empathize with your audience. This is why you need to remember your past emails, your blog posts, the information you have provided on the landing page etc etc. It is how you might be able to connect with them. When you write your email, be able to write it in a way that your email may be easily remembered and then your email marketing campaign can be effective and you can get the results you want and need.

Email newsletters have become a favored advertising tool to drive traffic to websites. But it can also be a great way to establish relationships and build your business. The following tips should help you take advantage of this effective advertising strategy.

Be Concise: An email newsletter is best suited for people who don't have a lot of time to go through everything. It could save you the trouble and effort to comb through web pages and make your point. Just click on a link, copy the link, paste the link in the text box in the newsletter and hit submit. Do the same for each article, post, ad, etc.

Focus on what's Important: you could be sending messages to people who would like to hear from you, so focus on what's important to them. People hate reading long and boring content that they have to remember numerous times. To avoid this, only focus on what's important to people.

Get to the point: If you have to explain everything in the newsletter, chances are people won't want to read it. Use bullet points, italics, etc. to highlight key points. Be brief and to the point. People would rather receive a short email rather than a long one with irrelevant content.

Have a catchy title: It should be catchy enough to keep people' attention but brief. A catchy title can surely get people to open the email.

Avoid Spam-Like Messages: Don't mix content with ads or promotional offers. People hate it. Instead focus on relevant content. It's a common fact that people tend to open and read emails more than they would pay attention to an advertisement.

The importance of writing emails to your customers or subscribers cannot be understated. A well-crafted email is a sales tool that can make people buy products or services every time. Writing effective emails or newsletters is an art, therefore, which can be mastered through consistent practice. A well-crafted newsletter can result in more sales if properly sent out to your customers.

24. Email Marketing - A Simple Guide to Writing Emails That Deliver

To have a successful email marketing campaign you need to make a well designed email but if your email is boring and unoriginal, then you could get no response from your subscribers. Make a risk free approach and a well designed email could lead to more response and more sales.

If your email creative is boring and unoriginal, you may not be able to catch your subscribers attention. So, the first thing to be done is to create an email creative that is both well designed and is exciting. If you would not think that an email creative is both well designed and is exciting, then you have got to think again.

There is a real time feedback system in your email marketing campaign. The more risk-tolerant emails you create, the more you will probably benefit from your email campaign. The more exciting the email, the more you can get a response from your subscribers.

The feedback feature within your email marketing campaign is an important tool for you to catch your subscribers attention and also to understand what is really interesting for your subscribers.

It is a feedback system, where your subscribers email address is the input box and you have posted the review of the email. The more you write about the email you received from your subscribers, the more you can know what is really interesting to your subscribers. You should be able to create another email campaign and another marketing campaign and another marketing campaign can be based on what you have learned from the other email campaigns you have done before.

If you would simply write an email without any input from your customers at all. Again, you would simply see how many people responded to the email and how much they are interested by the email. This should enable you to determine the next email marketing campaign. Once you see how many people responded to the first email, you can then make a new email creative and send it to your subscribers as a beta email. This time, do your market research and try to tailor it to make it interesting for your customers. This is almost like comparing the placebo to the actual remedy. This can enable you to determine what the response is of the new and improved email campaign. Once you have determined the new email marketing campaign, and the third email marketing campaign after learning from these insights, you could send the new email campaign to the same area of your subscribers, and if there is a positive feedback, you can then keep on using the new email creative and send it to the same area of your subscribers and so on.

If your email creative is unoriginal, and boring, you will surely not be able to attract the interest of your subscribers. So, it is important that you must be a good writer. You can become an expert in email marketing and make an email marketing campaign for your company, or you can become an expert in writing email messages. There is a school of thought that says the former. However, if you are an expert in writing emails, then you can definitely be good at writing emails that are both interesting and original. Your subscribers could certainly be interested by the emails that you send them. And your email creative skills may certainly help you a lot in attracting the interest of your subscribers.

One important thing to do is to include text as well in your email marketing campaign.

This may help your subscribers to read your emails. Instead of just images, they should be able to see the text. This can definitely help in conveying your ideas clearly. And it can help your readers in understanding your message in the best way possible. And the text can help you understand what you are talking about.

So, you can write emails in the best way possible using both text as well as images. Just be sure that your emails contain both. It would be a shame to send out poor emails. But, if you have to do it in a certain way, then you can write your emails using the text. And if you are confident that your emails are going to be effective, then you can include both the images and the text. It is just a matter of doing your best in writing your emails.

25. One Time Offers

Having an email newsletter can really help your business grow. If you use email marketing you have the opportunity to send emails out to your list. They are very similar to newspaper and magazine advertisements that you have seen with the addition of the logo and text. For those that do not know, email marketing involves the sending of emails to a list of subscribers who have given permission to receive such emails. These emails can either be one time only promotions or be sent out periodically. It is very important that you try to reach as many people as you can with your email marketing campaign.

There are many benefits for you if you use email marketing. This can make people aware of your business and that is the biggest advantage. When your subscribers get to know your business, then they could be more willing to purchase from your business. The best part is that this can all be automated. All that you need to do is have the ability to create HTML emails which can easily be done by anyone that knows HTML.

Your email marketing campaign can contain one time offers which are targeted to a specific group of customers. For example, you can offer them one time deals which only work with a specific product or service. This might increase the conversion rate from your email marketing campaign because there are many times when people can read the email for information but could not make a purchase because it was not what they were looking for at that time. This means that you have another chance to try to persuade them to purchase from you. For this reason it is very important that you take this option.

In a standard email campaign, you can usually only make blanket offers that work for many people but nothing that can convert on everyone. That's because there is a relatively low degree of customization. For example, you could offer free shipping on items but if you have unique or narrow-scoped products, you may see a lot of people ignore your email campaigns. This is very unlikely to work because you are offering something that they are not interested in. It's often a better strategy to cater your emails to specific groups of subscribers.

The only way to make your email marketing campaigns work is to target your audience appropriately. This means that you should only send out the emails to people who are interested in the products and services that you offer. This is because your email marketing campaign is for the customers that have already indicated that they are interested in your products. For example, if you purchase an opt-in list then you can be fairly certain that the subscribers have expressed interest in the products and services that you offer. If you purchase a raw list then you may have a little more difficulty. If you will be creating one-time offers, then you may have no difficulty at all with this aspect.

The trick is that you can find a list of people who are looking for your products and who will not be interested in anything else. In order to find these people you can offer people with offers which are related to their interest. You can offer them one time offers and free shipping because these are the two things that you offer them on average.

26.5 Ways to Build a Valuable Email List

This article will tell you the best ways to build your email list.

1. Offer A Free Report

To get people to sign up you have to give them something. What you give them won't make them use your email list, but it'll get them used to giving you their email address. The more helpful you are with your free report, the more people can sign up for your list.

The two common ways to give something away are via RSS Feeds, and via a Free Video.

You can send a message to your email list that'll allow them to get the free report via an RSS feed. The feed can tell them what day it is, which means they know it'll be coming. You can also put a link in your email to get the free report. The last step is telling them to check their email.

2. Send Useful Content

The content of your email comes first. You want to know what the people on your email list are interested in. If the content you're sending isn't important, your email list won't be interested in it. Your email list should notice the difference.

3. Give Your Email List The Ability To Register

Give your email list the ability to register for your newsletter. If they have to give you their email address to sign up, then you can set up autoresponders and send them your newsletter automatically. This is a very important part of building your email list.

4. Take The Time To Do This Right

This whole process can be very overwhelming. There are so many facets, and so many steps. This is just the beginning of the journey of building your email list. Take the time to do it right. You'll be building a list of real active subscribers who are interested in hearing from you. The more effort you put in, the more money you'll make.

5. Make It Easy

Before you start sending your newsletter out, you want to make it as easy as possible for people to sign up. You want to make it as painless as possible. If they have to do too much work, they won't want to sign up. If you make the process as painless as possible, people will be more likely to sign up.

Email marketing can be extremely profitable. Make it easy for people to sign up and give them a high value newsletter on your subject. Make it painless as possible and you'll see the results of a long term relationship.

27.4 Tips For Creating a Highly Effective Newsletter

The following advice is for people who might be getting in a little bit of grief from their friends and family because they are still sending out that pesky email newsletter that isn't really making them any money.

What's that? You've stopped sending out emails? You've stopped posting your articles online? Well if you haven't learned to improve your work, stop sending it! If you're still doing that, you're losing some of your readers, and you're likely wasting your time and your energy.

There are two kinds of email newsletter. First, there's that annoying kind where you never update on time, your subject lines are always boring, and the newsletter looks like it was written by a bunch of high school kids who are bored and feel like sharing a bunch of marketing material.

And then there's a better kind, the kind that people actually read, where you update them on a product or a service or some new information that you think might be of interest to them. In this kind of newsletter, you actually update them often and the newsletter looks more professional.

What you want to do is send a regular type newsletter that looks professional, and is updated often.

Here's how to do it: When you're writing your newsletter, don't just keep it short. Think about having a certain number of articles that can go into the newsletter. Maybe every other week? Two articles every week? Or even once a month? Think about having one or two testimonials in your newsletter, and then include some more content that discusses the product or service. The more you do it, the more you're likely to see the results.

When you're writing your newsletter, don't just have just one article. Instead, have a mini series of articles that discuss the benefits of the product or service in depth, and then provide some extra information that addresses problems that the product or service might help address. You might have a whole article on how this product or service is different from the competition, how it has something that the competition doesn't, and then use the testimonials in the newsletters to show them how it really works.

When you're writing your newsletter, don't just write some text on the page. Instead, spend some time writing a powerful headline that grabs their attention and makes them want to read the entire newsletter. You can even use this tactic to convince people to buy the product itself. For instance, if you're writing a newsletter about a high-end audio product, write an article that gives a brief history of how this product came to be, how it's been designed and manufactured, and then provide some testimonials that demonstrate how good it really is.

And speaking of writing, don't just write the newsletter with the autoresponder on auto-pilot. If you write with the autoresponder on auto-pilot, you'll be so busy writing that you may forget to include the extra content. Instead, write on a regular basis, adding other marketing materials to it, such as your website, marketing materials, email campaign, articles, and more. This might ensure that you don't miss any opportunities to promote the product, which should ensure that you'll do more business. You could even include a bio of your company occasionally, but only occasionally.

Conclusion

So there you have it. Three tips that you can use when creating your newsletter. The more articles you write in your newsletter, generally the more the chances are that people can click on it to find out more. On the whole, the more email messages you write (up to a certain degree) and the more captivating they are, the more the chances are that the people who received them could forward them to their friends. And the more auto responders you set up, the more the chances are that you'll make more sales. However, don't overdo it!

28. How Much Content Should I Include in My Newsletter?

When you're thinking about starting a newsletter that's going to give your business something that it doesn't currently have, one of the questions that are going to come to your mind is probably "How much content can I fit in this newsletter?" While the question "How much content can I fit in" is something that is going to be in your head constantly, there is actually a really easy answer to this.

The most important thing that you need to remember is that you should always focus on the quality of the newsletter. The quantity is something that you can have to deal with on your own.

When you're writing your newsletter, don't ever be afraid to talk about what you're doing. When you do this, you are going to be able to give your subscribers everything that they need to make a decision to open your newsletter. By giving them all the information that they need, it can also help in building trust with your subscribers. When you're talking about the benefits of your products, don't be afraid to talk about them. When you do this, you are going to be able to let your subscribers know about the benefits of buying your products.

While you are doing this, your readers are also going to be motivated to make a purchase if you do it right. Also, make sure you don't talk about yourself all the time. When you do this, your readers could start thinking that you're only interested in making money for yourself instead of building a long term relationship with them. Be proud of your products and be proud of your company but don't make it seem obvious.

Another thing that you need to remember is to never forget about the idea of educating your subscribers. In the newsletter, you are going to talk about things like how to install your products and all the troubles and information that they should need to know. This is actually something that is going to help your readers to make sense of what you are telling them. You're going to be able to pass along these things in a simple and simple way.

So remember, you need to always focus on the quality of the newsletter and forget about the quantity. When you do that, you may be able to build a great trusting relationship with your readers and that might help you to make a lot of money in the long run. And, if you have a ton to write, simply redirect them to the article page so they can read all of it and even read another great article on your website after that.

29. How to Improve Your Skills

Understand your target market. Who are you selling to? What problems are they facing? What are the obstacles in your path to help them? Once you've identified your target market you can write more effective emails.

Know what works and what doesn't. Once you've nailed down what works and what doesn't it's time to test your emails with other emails, print and postcards, telephone calls and face to face encounters. In order to do this you need data. Which email worked better than another email. Which email did more business than the others? Which email did the best than with the others? This will probably allow you to write emails with greater effectiveness, whereas effectiveness can allow you to grow your list.

Get into the habit of regularly testing your emails. This will almost always allow you to understand your market better and draw certain conclusions. In time, you may see which emails work best and most effectively and you can start to see consistent results from them. This in turn could allow you to write your emails more effectively and effectively can allow you to grow your list.

Email marketing is still, and always will be, a relatively inexpensive way of reaching a lot of people in a relatively short space of time. Think about it. When you compare it to the many forms of advertising available, email marketing can provide you with far more information in far less time, with far less cost and with far more potential profit. Which leads us to our next point...

Use your free time wisely - Your time is precious. It is vital that you make the most of it. Don't let your free time be wasted watching videos, reading blogs, following people, signing up to people's lists, and browsing social networking sites. Spend your time doing things that might help you grow your business. If you don't, you may never learn how to build your own list. Spend time online learning how to write email messages, how to write effective autoresponder messages, how to write a Landing Page, how to write a Squeeze page, and how to build a list. Don't let your time be wasted. If you have a few hours each week spent in total control of your business you could easily be earning hundreds of dollars a month. I have spent less than an hour in total to control my business and it has enabled me to rapidly build my list in less than a year. So use your free time to do what needs to be done.

Be very cautious when doing business with Internet marketers that are unknown. Be very careful what you do, and don't do, and what you accept if you don't have to pay for their services. If you don't know who they are or that they are reputable, don't do business with them. Understand that a negative rating in Yelp does not in any way mean that the individual you opted into their list is reputable. Even if the individual you opted into their list has a zero rating in the Yelp rating system, your email and autoresponder messages can still be rated as spam and you can still be billed for their services.

The bottom line is it is imperative that you understand the power of filters to help protect you from being marked as spam, even if you have a zero rating from Yelp and zero rating from other rating services. In my experience, I have found that I am marked as spam by the ISP I bounced at a rate of 5 to 10 times higher. There is nothing like total control to protect you from spam, there are numerous reasons why the ISP that you are opted into could rate you as spam, but in order to fully understand how to keep you from being marked as spam, I recommend that you understand this: If you are willing to pay for your goods and services, and opt into their mailing list without exception, you can not be marked as spam. The biggest reason why you are not marked as spam is because your filters have a zero rating on you, and even if you get a few spam messages, it is expected because your filters have a zero rating on you. When you understand the filter business that I've described, it may give you the confidence you need to go out and try new businesses, and to stay opt in to the list of the individuals that you respect and believe in.

If you want your Internet business to be successful, don't ever do anything that requires you to be marked as spam.

30. Using Double Opt In

I've tried email marketing. Done it. Bought it. Sold it. I'm aware of all that is requisite for making an effective, quality email campaign. And I've got good news! It's not too difficult to set up and maintain. It is, however, time consuming. I don't know anybody who doesn't have at least one, if not more, projects to juggle, clients to appease, and partners to please. So this process for a well established professional is time consuming, and it doesn't have the greatest ROI if you do it the wrong way!

Like many marketers, when I receive an email from my business, I make the assumption that it is either a solicitation for a product or an offer to my business. In neither case is it a solicitation for an audience. For me, and this is just a hunch, I assume it has something to do with my business. My assumption is wrong. If I open the email, it is usually because I got an email from my friend, who also got an email from his friend. I think we are all like that.

In order to keep from getting the B-team treatment by the spam filters, I keep my email lists, or subscriber lists, and subscriber lists of contacts to a minimum. I hate that. I don't keep lists of email addresses of everyone who contacted me with something. Why would I? I like being able to build a relationship with my customers. The thing is, I don't hate them. I know, and they know, that emailing me is a form of solicitation. So, what am I to do?

A good idea I see being proposed, if it works for you and your business, is to just send your email to your friend lists. If your list of friends is large, you can easily keep them all. Just don't be surprised when you get a lot of responses to your email. You may even get some sales. Be prepared though. There is a learning curve.

But there is a problem with this approach. People may often respond to your friend's lists. If you do this regularly, people may recognize your email. As a result, you might want to make sure that your emails get through the filters as well. You want your recipient to think that your email is not a solicitation. In order to accomplish this, you may want to use double opt-in.

How do I double opt in?

In order to double opt in, you should want to send a confirmation email to anyone who responds to your first email. This is standard industry practice, and this can ensure that the sender has confirmed their identity. This should avoid you getting bounced emails and other problems that can arise from people answering your initial email.

This double opt-in can also help you keep the other parties on your list. Your recipient may choose to unsubscribe from the list or delete their inbox, and they might want to keep the people on their list. Also, your customer list may have people who may be interested in a service you offer, or a product you sell. This could keep the price of the message high. This can make it more likely that the recipient should be interested in your message.

Don't include "free" in your subject line. Most SPAM filters read the subject line and filter your email. If you read the whole subject line, then you can decide for yourself if "free" should be in the subject line or not.

Another thing is to avoid using words in the subject line that are commonly found in SPAM filters like "free", "click here", "entertaining" etc. The filter will likely "learn" to recognize the words. If you use a word that's commonly used in SPAM filters, you may end up in the spam folder and your email won't be read.

The last thing is to use the standard template that the majority of email clients and software use now. I usually like to use "Welcome" as my first line and put it in the standard template. But the first paragraph could usually depend on what they are used to seeing.

The basic rule is to use words that are a natural match for the recipient's email client or software. Don't use spam-like words like "free" or "limited offer", avoid using lots of punctuation or symbols or using lots of asterisks, circles, triangles or diamonds. So, the only things that are a bit out of place are the words "welcome" and "my name is ___".

You can use the standard template or personalize it as you like. I usually put in my first name, which is just short for mine). Then I put in my company name. Then I use their name or their title. Then I use some of the other phrases that I've used in the past in articles or newsletters or wherever. And then I've gone back and deleted some of the other phrases to clean up the form and make it the way I like it.

31. Email Marketing Tips

To build a huge yet responsive email list, you can send a confirmation message that includes a welcome email that tells your subscribers to click on the link inside the message to confirm their subscription to the list.

Why?

You want to get people to go through the link included in the welcome message rather than risk them marking the message as spam and deleting it.

Now that you've got them to go through the link inside the message, you now want to make sure they also click on the link inside the confirmation message. This is why a confirmation message should contain a welcome message from your list that also contains a link.

Remember the link is both a way for them to confirm their subscription and a way for you to allow them to continue to receive emails from you if they decide to unsubscribe after clicking through the link.

The welcome message also includes a confirmation message for your list, which contains a link to continue to be able to receive emails from you.

Afterwards, when they click on the link, you automatically continue to send them an email. The only thing you are not allowing them to continue to receive emails from you are unsubscribe requests and other messages, unless they decide to add those to their whitelist.

The other reason you should have a confirmation message is to give them the ability to change their settings in the options sent with the message. Most autoresponders do not allow you to easily change settings or opt out. You should allow your list to easily change preferences in your email.

Remember, your welcome message should also contain a message that also contains a link to opt in to the list, since many might put the white list message after the confirmation message. You can also include this link to let them know they have just subscribed to your list.

This is a lot of email marketing to send to your subscribers, but you can automate the process by using these basic email marketing strategies.

To get a good response rate and a high response from your list, the best strategy is to only send very high value, very high relevance messages. If your content is not relevant to your subscribers' interests, you might struggle to get a high response and could get a low response, or none at all.

You should always keep your message content related and valuable to your subscribers. If your message is not valuable, you should also make sure your list has some way of deleting your messages without you. You should send the same message to your list about 6 times.

As an example, say you have a membership site and one of the membership options is for a free newsletter. You should try to send one free newsletter per week. The first week you should try to send 1 email, the second 2 emails, the third 3 emails and so on. Do not send more than 3 emails per week to your list.

How to make your emails more engaging?

1. Content is the essence of content marketing. So, it is not only the product that must be informative, but also its content. The quality of the product and its content is the reason why people buy a product or subscribe to a newsletter.

2. The product must be useful. It is not important how many links are in the newsletter, but rather whether the product is useful and appropriate. There should be no links or other extraneous content outside of the necessary. The product should be relevant and useful, presented in a clear and understandable manner.

3. The newsletter does not always have to be written in HTML format. It can also be written in plain text, and in pretty-much any technology. The only thing that matters is that the newsletter meets the needs of the subscribers.

4. The newsletter has to be delivered and displayed in a quick manner. It should not take too much time and resources.

5. It should also be interesting. The content of the newsletter should be similar to the themes of the readers. Therefore, if the subscribers are divided into groups or cohorts, they can be exposed to the same themes or subjects. If the themes are relevant, and also the topic is relevant to the subscriber, the number of engagement and the revenue generally goes up. Email newsletters can be used as a tool for increasing revenues and subscribers as stated above. From a legalized standpoint, the major difference between a newsletter and spam is that a newsletter is permission based.

There are different approaches to increase revenues. The only difference between those approaches is the approach to take. However, no matter how you use it, if the newsletter is not interesting, or not relevant or not useful, you may not increase revenues. You may just end up decreasing revenues.

Sell Without Sounding Salesy!

Many people think they can just slap their name and web link on an eBook and make a sale. I suggest you do extensive research on what sort of competitors your potential customers use. Don't create a sales pitch for your software as this may come off as fake and you may lose credibility. Your ebook or software must be informative and not like a sales letter for your software- this could bring people to click through your link.

You must be careful with your keywords. This is an important part of SEO and search engine optimization. The more specific you can get with your keyword, the better. It can also help with the design of your page. Long keywords such as navigation or other more descriptive terms are good. Make your pages easy to navigate. Include a call to action. This means you must tell your customer what is to be done. A good place to place a call to action is near the bottom of your page. Another important part of SEO is the title.

Make your title catchy and related to the content of your page. Don't overdo it, keep it natural.

Affiliate Marketing + Email Marketing!

32. How to Make Money With Affiliate Programs

If you're looking for ways to make money online, one of the easiest ways to get started is with affiliate programs. They are easy to set up, can make you a lot of money in affiliate marketing, and you can sign up for free. In short, you promote your affiliate's product or service through a link, and if someone clicks on the link and buys it, you make money.

In order to set up an affiliate program, you may need a few things. First, you would need to choose what industry you want to promote in.

Within the industry you can have many product lines to choose from. However, in order to reduce the workload on yourself, it's best to choose a single product in which you feel comfortable promoting.

Once you have made your choice, the next thing you'll need is a domain name that has to be easy to remember, and is easy to search. You can get a domain name for free or cheap, or by subscribing to a plan for an all-in-one website builder with an in-build email marketing tool, blog, and other functions that could help you promote the affiliate product.

In order to make money with your affiliate program, you should promote it. It's easy to set up a website, the hard part is to get people to trust it, and eventually click on and purchase from your affiliate links. Setting it up is the easy part. Promoting your program is where your core competency comes in.

You don't have to sell physical products -- many affiliate programs sell e-courses, seminars, training programs, software, or other subscription plans like a membership, where people pay a monthly fee in order to receive benefits from the program.

Within your affiliate program, you can have different offer choices. You can choose to offer different products from different companies. Each product has a different amount, or commission, of money, or pay out %. You can set different amounts for different products within an industry.

You can also set different payout % values for different products within the same industry. For example, if you choose an industry where you can promote weight loss products, you can set different values for pay out % than for products that promote prostate health products, etc.

With this, you'll be able to create a variety of income streams. You can promote hundreds of products within the same industry and get diverse income streams. Or, you can set pay out % values for a single product, like a VPN connection from a single provider, so that people who buy it can get different pay out % values depending on the channel or the link that they use.

Another way to make money with your program is by using pay per lead. You can get paid $1.50 for each person who fills out a form. This is less common than the aforementioned. You would generally need to create an account with a website that does pay per lead. The main difference is that you might get paid once per customer. It's a simple way to promote multiple products, so long as you can get a good checkout conversion.

33. Affiliate Marketing - 4 Factors to Consider When Looking For a Product

There are many reasons why people could choose to sell products online. One of the popular reasons is that there is very little capital outlay necessary to get started. Since there is not much expense, many people see it as an easy way out. However, in order to make money online there are a few things that you must be aware of.

First, before you decide to sell any products online, you should do some research on the market. For example, try checking and researching websites like the major search engines to find out what the demand is for such products. This could give you a good idea about what you should be marketing. If the market is high, then it means that there is demand for such products. However, don't forget to research the level of competition as well. At the end of the day, most niches will already be saturated, at least to an extent, so quality and rigor of your promotions is key to success.

Second, the market that you choose to start with must be profitable. The reason for this is that you want to get your feet wet so that you can master the art of marketing. For example, if there is no demand for such a product, then there is no point in you marketinging such a product unless you have a competitive advantage in terms of reaching the desired customer base. This depends on the exclusivity of your marketing channel. For example, say you have a large following on a video hosting website or social media. Think of social media influencers. Then, the product that you promote can be marketed within your existing channel to your followers. In that case, you would want to make sure that your existing audience has an affinity with the type of product you choose to promote. For example, it wouldn't make sense to promote car tires on a beauty channel.

Lastly, you would need to decide how you are going to sell your product. Are you simply redirecting your customers to a funnel or landing page that leads to your affiliate seller's product page, or are you actually fulfilling the order? In the case of affiliate marketing, the former is likely to be the case.

These are some of the things that you need to do in order to make money online with affiliate marketing. This is a lucrative way of making money as it does not need to cost you a penny to get started. Moreover, it is possible for you to start marketing at no cost as well if you do not have a website, following, or a product. Think of it this way: as an affiliate marketer, your golden formula is to share your affiliate product with as many people as possible, and this can be achieved by various means.

There is a certain formula for making money in the internet market. There are some factors that you need to consider when you are looking for a lucrative market. You may need to consider the following:

1. What is the Demand for the product?

This is the most important factor for your success in the market. You should consider what kind of product people are looking for. You may need to be able to find out what the demand is for the product. If there is a demand for a certain product then you may have a target market that could make money for you.

2. How well does the company supply the product?

You may need to consider what kind of service the company provides. Will you be dealing with live chat, email support, product shipping or a system of links to the product that you are selling? You will need to have adequate knowledge of these factors that could affect the number of sales that you will be getting.

Also, don't forget about shipping. Free shipping is a great way to increase conversions. It's often much better to simply add the shipping margin to the product price and list it as free shipping, which attracts customers. In addition to free shipping, fast shipping is just as important if not more. Labeling the product with "fast shipping" or "quick delivery" can significantly boost sales.

3. Is there a money back guarantee?

You will need to consider the money back guarantee provided by the company you are looking into promoting. If there is a guarantee given then you will want to make sure that the guarantee will be valid. You may need to make sure that you can ask for your money back if there is something that is not correct about the product.

These are some of the factors that you may need to consider when you are looking for a lucrative market. You might need to make sure that you keep your eyes open and ensure that you are choosing a lucrative market that can give you the best chance of making money. Once you have found a lucrative market then you might need to ensure that you focus on it and keep your eyes on it to avoid wasting time.

4. What type of people would purchase your product?

Identifying and picturing your target audience clearly is super important to ensure that you maximize conversions and click-through rates. Knowing your target audience could enable you to prime and prepare them for the product so that they feel attracted to your product before you actually present it to them.

34. Dealing With Affiliate Partners

One of the best and easiest ways to make money online is to set up a website and then promote affiliate programs for others. Now you need to realize something. Most of the affiliate programs out there are just designed to send you commissions for signing up new members or selling products. They don't give a damn about teaching you how to make money online.

They give you the tools and the money is sent to your paypal account. If you really think about it, you are out on your own, without much assistance from the affiliate program owner. The affiliate program owner generally is not harmed by partners who don't convert lots of sales (unless they promote the product in a harmful way). Besides, it's hard for them to know who will end up as a top-performing affiliate partner and who won't. That's why many affiliate partners will grant permission to sell their products to anyone pleases, knowing that it's a numbers game for them.

There are some good programs out there and you really need to research them. You don't want to sign up with one that doesn't give you a decent income because you can easily find those.

Most of these programs are set up so that you can get the most amount of traffic with the least amount of effort. Do you think an affiliate program owner is going to give you a list if you can hardly get just 3 visitors to their site with your website and you are the one driving them there? That is crazy!

Some of these affiliate programs could even pay you per click or per lead. If you aren't getting any traffic it doesn't make sense to them. They have to get leads if they are going to be successful in the long term. It's just a numbers game for them.

I have found the most success and income streams by doing research. Don't rush into things without doing your homework. Most of the best affiliate programs are set up so that you really do need to do your research.

Don't rush into things with a plan and then find that they don't pay much and you don't get paid in the long term. That's not to say that there are no good ones out there. I am still just as attracted to many of the ones I looked at as I was before.

Take your time to read up on the affiliate programs and the owner. Research is crucial in your success!

35. Online Affiliate Marketing: The Battle Cry

It is a very simple fact that most people who want to learn affiliate marketing get caught up in all the hype and confusion. They want to know the answer to the big question, "How much money can I make as an affiliate marketer?"

The simple answer is, "It all depends". There is no simple formula, and no number that says you will be able to count on 100% success. This is one of the big secrets of affiliate marketing, that people tend to shy away from. If you truly want to succeed as an affiliate marketer, you have to treat it like a real business.

I want to preface this by saying that affiliate marketing is one of the best ways to make money online. The money is fantastic, and it is easy. And the work involved is minimal. But, it is still work. In fact, one of the most honest assessments one can make about affiliate marketing is that it is the most work-intensive way to make money online.

Why? Because you have to spend hours and hours at the computer, trying to get traffic. I remember when I first started, I spent so many hours in traffic, it was taking a toll on my family. The truth is, it does take a toll, and if you let it, it could eventually shorten your lifespan.

A good way to do this is to have a way to reduce labor, that is acceptable, that also allows you to earn money. I recommend you do not use your family's time or finances to build a business. You know better. So, find a way to reduce labor while still getting paid.

How would you like to be paid? Well, you make the money. You send traffic to the merchants website and you get paid a commission, anywhere from 10%-80%. So, you know that you reduce labor while still making the commission.

Now that you know that affiliate marketing is a real business, you need to find a good affiliate company to promote. I recommend you find an affiliate company that pays at least 40%-50% commissions. You do not have to be a rocket scientist to figure out that a high commission percentage is good. However, if the commission is too high, beware that the product may not be selling.

The other option is to get a little more advanced with your affiliate marketing, and create your own website and use affiliate directories. You have to pay a little more for your products, but the return on your investment is often better.

Use affiliate directories to promote your website and products. Remember, you want to make sure that the affiliate products you are promoting are worth the time and effort to promote. Stay laser-focused and don't get tied down in details. Look for the simplest methods to solve a problem. Seek help online. Spending your time effectively can help avoid fatigue and pitfalls.

36. How to Get More Clicks to Your Affiliate Products

Making money through affiliate programs is probably the easiest way to make money online -- if you know how to connect with customers on any given platform. It doesn't really matter if you're on social media or on any other platform for that matter. I've even seen people who sold tons of affiliate products by word of mouth.

The affiliate programs offer the ability to promote your chosen products, the chosen platform, chosen audience, in an automated fashion, and in many cases you don't have to have a product to sell.

This is an ideal business for beginners since you can start making money right away without having to develop a product. The concept is that someone can sign up on your affiliate program and you can send them a promotional email, and if they decide to buy then you can receive a commission. This is great for people who don't want to develop a product since they won't have to spend time developing a product and can focus on other things.

Affiliate marketing can also be a very good way to get started if you are not interested in developing your own sales channel. However you have to realize that there is usually a fairly high failure rate in affiliate marketing. This is mainly due to people not reading the details inside the programs and not researching the product but promoting the product anyway. In addition, you ought to know and have the right channels to promote your affiliate products! Having the link is the easy part, but driving traffic, targeted traffic, is the hard part!

Another reason people fail in affiliate marketing is because they don't do enough targeting. It is possible to make a lot of money in affiliate marketing by targeting the right keywords, but you really need to understand what keywords are and how they affect the sales process.

In order to make a lot of money in affiliate marketing you likely need to send targeted traffic to your website. Without traffic you're probably not going to make any sales. Targeted traffic basically means the traffic that is not too competitive and has recently bought something before.

If you send traffic that has recently purchased something else, then they are more likely to exit your site and they won't likely be able to buy anything. Most people don't buy on their first visit to your website, so you really need to send targeted traffic to your site every day.

Another strategy that can be used in affiliate marketing is using your affiliate link to get traffic to your website. When someone clicks on your affiliate link and goes to the parent website, you may want to be able to link them back to your website. You can get this link by placing a simple HTML code on your affiliate program site, or you can purchase a link database that will allow you to place a link on every page of your website. You need to be sure to not link directly to the product though, you want to link to a page where you can link to the product that you are promoting. This can save you money in advertising and get more clicks to your site.

One way to get more targeted traffic is to create more blogs. You need to create a blog that is specific to the product you are promoting. You can do this by writing about it's benefits and how it can help your customers. You can also write articles on it's benefits and then place the link in your blog post. The more blog posts you make, the more traffic you could get. If you do this well you should get more sales.

One of the biggest obstacles to your success as an affiliate is the amount of time you are willing to spend on your business. You may find many affiliates who will tell you that you do not need to put in a lot of time to get the results that you are looking for. However, this should not be taken at face value, because time is required to become an expert at virtually anything. If you want to achieve financial freedom, then you cannot ignore the time you spend. In fact, money may not be a worry for you anytime soon, but you should still put in the right amount of time to improve your chances of success. Hence, you should spend a lot of time learning how to promote your products more effectively as well as actually promoting them.

There are many affiliate marketing programs out there but you have to make sure that you know what works and what does not. Most of the products that you may find out there will not fit your online niche and it will likely require some technical skills to use it.

Most affiliate programs require that you have your own website or blog. However, if you do not have your own website or blog, then you may have to join other websites that can provide you with a platform for free.

There are many web hosting companies that can provide you with a platform so that you can get started with your online business. You may need to make sure that you choose a web host that is reliable and is not just making a full scam out of your online business. There are many hosting companies that also do website design. Such companies can provide you with website templates and there are many templates that are in use by affiliate marketers.

However, there are also many websites that are just full of scam because they do not give you what you need. You should check the websites that you are going to use before you sign up. You may be able to tell the truth from the false websites if there is someone asking for your money but doesn't have a full set of well-integrated features, from the website builder itself to fulfillment and analytics.

You may need to check their policies before you sign up. If you have questions about their policies then just contact the owner of the site directly.

In closing, you may find that affiliate marketing is a very lucrative online business. However, you have to put in the right amount of time for your business. There are many things that you have to do before you can see money coming into your account.

37. Why Pay for Affiliate Marketing?

Many times you can find that the best affiliate program is the one that is free. You would certainly not want to pay for an affiliate program. You have to be careful about this. There is no such thing as a free lunch.

However, there are many times when paying for an affiliate program is the better choice. Let's talk about what some of these are.

1. Paying For A Program Provides A Point Of Competency.

When you pay for your affiliate program, you are providing information. They need to know that I accepted your commission for this reason. That you paid for this reason. So that they understand that your reputation is important to them. It helps them to see that they must be sure that the products they are promoting are indeed of quality.

2. You Can Select Better Products.

Your payment could help them to be certain that the product is good. If the products are good, they could be more assured that they can convince their customers that the product is of quality. A decent affiliate program can save you time and money.

3. They Can Select Your Customers.

As you sell your products, your visitors become your customers. Your visitors can become your customers for one reason: They were interested in the product that you were promoting, and your priming of the product resonated with them. They go on to become your customers because you recommended them to buy the product and it worked. Having a wider range or a more specialized range of products to promote could give you a broader choice of customers you can select to sell to.

38. Do You Want to Get Results Fast Or Slowly?

So you think you have what it takes to be a successful internet marketer?

Unless you've passed through several learning curves, you probably do not have what it takes to be a successful internet marketer. Affiliate marketing is not as easy as just finding a good product. Vendors need affiliates because they don't have the marketing expertise to sufficiently grow and scale their product, which is where you come in. You are the one who must figure out the marketing part. That's going to be the hard part. So finding the right product is one thing, but being able to promote it is a whole different matter. That's where your value comes in.

If you think you can simply post a link and sell a product, the reality is that most-likely, you can't do that. You can't just look at a product, decide to be the vendor, and just sell. You need to know something about the product you are looking at and what it does. You need to have used the product, so you know how it can benefit your customers. You need to know what your customers want, and what they need. You need to know the size of your target market, and what your sales copy should be. All these factors play into the final equation of your success as an affiliate.

If you lack knowledge, your chances of succeeding are slim. People can see you as not caring about your customers, as if you don't even care about the product. If you lack passion, your sales could most-certainly be low.

Let me show you how you can potentially do this.

Product knowledge: It is possible to go through the sales page of a product, and decide to be the vendor, without knowing the product. It just takes a quick search on a search engine, using a few strings to look at the product, or use an app to look at the physical product. Many vendors make use of this way to get their names out there. Even though these methods are easy to use, they are not the fastest way to do it. So how do you speed up the process?

1. Knowledge: When you decide to be the vendor, it makes it easier to be excited about the product, and know the features of the product. This can be done with research on the product, and on the product itself. You need to have a basic understanding of what the product is all about, and how it will benefit your customers. This can be done by doing research on the product and product owners.

2. Passion: When you decide to be on the same wavelength as the vendor, it makes it easier to be motivated about the product, and you should be so passionate about it that you are willing to give up your time to promote it. Join a community with product enthusiasts and learn from them how to best sell that particular product, and what concerns customers have prior to making a purchase.

3. Research: When you decide to promote a product, this makes it easier to look at the sales page of the product, read the copy, look at the pictures, and make sure the product appeals to you. You need to be able to look at the product from the customer's perspective. If you can look at the product from the user's perspective, you might know more about how to promote it effectively. It could make it easier for you to write your promotion pieces. The more you are willing to do for your customers, the more customers you can get.

4. Time: When you decide to promote a product, it makes it easier to research the product, and get excited about it. It could make it easier for you to promote it if you can time it. Most new affiliates do not know how to time their promotion, and they do not know how to time it so that it goes well.

5. Commitment: When you decide to promote a product, it makes it easier for you to commit yourself to it when you feel passionate about selling it. If you are already promoting a product, it could make it easier for you to promote it again.

6. Discipline: When you decide to promote a product, it makes it easier for you to focus on it. The more disciplined you are, the more you can get results for your customers.

7. Optimism: When you decide to promote a product, it makes it easier for you to be optimistic about it when you bring an optimistic mindset to it. If you are not optimistic about it, you might not make much sales for it.

8. Willingness: Willingness is important because willpower is a little mental power that you have. It should make it easier for you to push yourself to finish your work.

You might have read that promoting a product is the easy part. That is true. But, if you have an affiliate marketing website, you may have to do more than promote a product. You may need to market your website consistently to get traffic. You may need to do SEO to get top rankings with web masters experts. You may need to submit articles to directories, submit blogs.

You can choose not to do any of these. You can choose to do nothing. But, you can only get results for doing what you do, unless you choose to outsource it. You could get results for promoting a product while sitting in the comforts of your own home, but only if the setup is right.

Now, you must decide how much commitment you are willing to put into your affiliate marketing business. If you have no commitment, you can only get results for promoting a product or creating a website. But, if you are willing to do some work, you can promote a product or create a website that is so much better.

Now, you must decide what choices you are willing to make.

39. Keeping Track Of Your Progress

Making money online is something that most people want to do and that's understandable. It's quick, easy and cheap to set up an online business. Unfortunately, it can be difficult to make money. After all, no one goes into a business with the intention of losing. The easiest way to make money online is to invest some of your money and some of your time in affiliate marketing.

Affiliate marketing is a marketing technique where the marketer agrees to promote someone else's product or service. There are many websites that provide a marketplace for vendors and for affiliates. To make money as an affiliate, you need to sign up and sometimes pay a certain fee. The website may then provide you with a website with links to the vendor's website.

Each time someone clicks on those links from your website and makes a purchase, you get a percentage of the sale. However, if someone clicks on the link but doesn't complete the purchase, you should still keep track of your link clicks so you have more data about your funnel. Sometimes, the product could be good but the product page or checkout page needs additional work. If your pages get too messy, you should consider simplifying the design.

It's easy to make money with affiliate marketing. Simply start a blog. You can use Wordpress if you have the opportunity to master it. Start writing articles about products or services that you have tested or used yourself and submit to different directories. You should also register your blog website with a search console so it is found on leading search engines.

As an affiliate marketer, you need to keep track of your visitors so that you can provide them with relevant offers. Start by identifying the kinds of visitors you've received and the website they came from. Then use a host of tools to track visitor demographics.

Be aware that there are some affiliate marketers that don't use these tools on their websites and rely on sheer hard work alone. Affiliate marketing is a great way to make money online and you don't even need your own products. There are many products out there that you can promote and generate sales from. There are also many marketing avenues you can take. Many people are using native or poster ads, article marketing and paid ads to generate sales. Many products can be found on Amazon and some products can be found on eBay.

Making money online isn't as difficult as some people make it out to be. You don't have to pay a huge sum of money for your website if you do it right. There are free marketing tools and you can start promoting products and earning commissions straight away. Making money online with affiliate marketing is possible, but you must begin training yourself.

40. Why Online Purchasing is Popular

You know the saying, 'an ounce of gold is better than a ton of sand'. That may be true in terms of monetary value, but when you consider the social value of a simple piece of jewelry it really becomes something better.

When you order a simple diamond band for your wedding ring or engagement ring it is simply a great way to show your devotion to your loved ones. A diamond band is certainly a symbol of love and romance. When you order a simple band it can be given to your friends or it can be given to your significant other.

People all over the world can receive a simple diamond band from you. This kind of a unique item could have lasting value. You can give away magnetic bracelets as well, which are quite popular and people love to wear them. It's the material, price, and design that matter most with these types of items.

In fact, many people are actually buying their first diamond engagement rings online, because they cannot find them locally. The main reason is cost, because the price tends to be more to produce a gold band and then sell it through an intermediary retail location. If you can cut out the middleman, then the customer saves money and it's a win-win situation. So imagine the cost of a gold band or platinum band when compared at a retail location or sold through an online vendor. The price difference could be 30% or more! Plus, you can select your favorite design online from thousands of options. It is a much better solution for many people.

Therefore, people are buying rings online because it is cheaper, more convenient and more practical. People are ordering custom designed bands for their specific design and the cost is about the same or less as if they were buying a local gold band. However, you should consider that a physical retailer does have two advantages: 1) the customer can see and try out the item in person and 2) the customer usually feels more assurance from a retail vendor in addition to a potential refund or warranty policy. Having said that, more and more online vendors are offering warranties and instituting return policies to make their offerings more attractive.

You can see why buying a simple band online is very popular because the items are affordable and people can receive them very easily. The products are designed in such a way that the customer has the satisfaction to receive the item they spent a lot of money on.

To date, there are already a lot of wholesale suppliers that offer wholesale wedding bands, engagement rings, and custom bands. You can get many different designs and products from these suppliers. The prices are reasonable and you get a quality product. All these benefits are available for online purchasing without any hassle or extra cost. This is very convenient because you do not have to run around trying to find a salesperson to help you in person.

When a customer orders an item from your site, the item is delivered directly to your customers. This is very easy, fast and very practical. You can deliver items anywhere in the world. You just have to know where to find a reliable courier company that can deliver your items to your customers. And the customers know that their items are delivered quickly and safely to them. The customers love it. They usually cannot wait to receive their items.

These reasons are why people love online purchasing of items.

41. Get Online Video Marketing Up and Running

One of the best ways to get traffic for your video is through social media. Video submission sites are also a great way to generate traffic for your videos and there is no better way to do that than to join social media networks with videos. Social media sites are one of the best ways to build an audience and get your videos discovered if you already have a following on them, but not the only means. You can post your affiliate link in the video description in most cases. In this article, we'll look at how you can make money through online video marketing.

Tip 1: Be Original

People love to be moved or entertained so make sure your video is something they haven't seen before. You don't have to reinvent the wheel, but you should make it exciting and different. Don't make your videos too serious or boring. Also, don't make them too promotional. Remember people are not going to click a button and send you money to your video account unless they really like you.

Tip 2: Do it Frequently

It is very important to do your video marketing regularly. Make sure you do it in an organized fashion. You want your marketing done regularly, so be consistent and present. Also, make sure you post them consistently. A video marketing schedule is a must so that your subscribers do not forget that you have videos posted.

Tip 3: Track Your Data

With video marketing, you need to know how many views your videos are getting. You need to know the demographics of your audience. You can do this by tracking your data. This is one of the best ways to make sure you aren't running ads or not marketing to certain audiences too much.

Tip 4: Use Video Extensions

You can use any of the video extensions available. They include play, fast forward, rewind, and similar. You can also add annotations and some of the annotations are video. Some of the annotation types include talking heads, graphics, screen captures and others. The most important is the video itself. The reason it is very important to use video is that it is the most viewed extension. Other extensions are liked, watched, visited, shared etc.

The last few years have seen a revolution in the way we use the internet. People are spending less time on traditional social media sites and more time on video sharing sites such as YouTube. And it isn't just the novelty of having a portal where your favourite shows, films and music videos are made that are making people turn to it. It's also the ability to create your own show, edit, add music and voice overs, then upload it to your channel for everyone to see and hear. It's the ability to have your video experience direct to your website and mobile phone.

So how can your business benefit from this revolution? With the ability to take your viewers on a virtual reality journey. The medium of video has come a long way since the first home video players hit the market. Now it's more common than not to come with a headset that you can wear to places like or just watch films on your sofa. That can provide a lead-listing effect, because you're essentially giving away something that can help you generate a lead for your business. Hence, if you can promote your affiliate links and products through a video sharing site, this could be an amazing way to market it.

Innovative business marketing isn't just restricted to YouTube. There's plenty of video hosting sites where you can put your videos. And you can potentially use services such as Vimeo, Viddler, Dailymotion, and Flickvid to host your videos. All of which have their own advantages. But YouTube is the go-to place for most people, for a good reason.

YouTube has also done a good job of making sure your videos stay live. If you leave your video up for too long, it'll automatically redirect to the YouTube website. And if you leave it up for too long, people could start to tune out. So it's a balancing act between redirecting too many people to the YouTube website and keeping the interest of those who do keep watching.

So it's a good place to be thinking of how you can incorporate videos into your business marketing. It's newbie friendly, so you don't have to relearn SEO. And it's got the right tone for start-up businesses. But that's not to say that there aren't other video sites out there that can be used.

The thing about YouTube is, it has the best search engine optimization. It was acquired by Google. This gives Google a vast amount of data on YouTube videos. And also YouTube is a video hosting site. So they have more video options than just YouTube.

Vimeo, Dailymotion, Viddler, and Flickvid are all video hosting sites (as of now). That's more options too.
Also you should ensure that the thumbnail is clear and relevant. Otherwise, people won't click on it.
The thumbnails need to be relevant to the video itself. So your thumbnail needs to relate to your video, and also the video itself. Otherwise, people may just disregard it. Videos could be very long or very short, it depends. Often, they're around 10 minutes or longer. So you still need to be careful about the thumbnail because that helps attract new viewers, especially those who are not already familiar with your channel.

Some video hosting sites have a thumbnail program. This is where the thumbnail comes into play. So you can get a high score. But you need to be careful about this also. Make sure that your thumbnail is relevant to your video. And the thumbnail needs to be relevant to you. If it's not, then people likely won't bother to click on it.

One last thing. YouTube is now also a video-sharing website. And other video sharing websites are able to embed your videos. So people watching your videos in these other video sharing websites can also share them. This is another way to spread your videos.

42. A Guide to Video Marketing

If you were to ask most internet marketers "what is the most effective form of marketing?" You would most likely receive different answers. You may find that some marketers love video marketing while others think it is optional. But, one thing is for sure if you ask me, no matter what form of marketing you are doing, you need to include video marketing in your marketing plan. Videos are simply much better at attracting people's attention than plain text. Besides, a professional video is a great way to introduce your company, website, or brand. Just make sure the quality of your videos are up to par.

Most marketers start off with a blog. A blog is great. A blog can be used to educate your clients about products or services you offer. But sometimes a blog can get boring and pointless. How do you market your blog when you can't say anything new or unique every day? This is where video marketing comes in. You can start sending out videos on your blog. This gets your clients watching your videos. This is how you can keep your clients coming back for more videos.

Here is an example. Say you run a business offering tickets to exotic destinations. You can explain the process of purchasing a ticket on your site, get them full of questions about the different departure times and cities, and get them in the know about all the perks of staying at your resort. Then you can end the video with a final call to action for them to purchase the ticket, book a flight or drive back to their office to make their reservation. You can use the video to give them the lowdown on the different cities and departure times and the perks of booking in advance.

Why is video marketing the best form of marketing?

- Visibility. Since people could watch videos as much as they may read, you can get your message out to thousands of people without using pay per click advertising.

- Cost. It's free to create the videos and you could be surprised by how many people may watch your videos.

- Frequency. Use your videos to send your message out to your target market twice per week. That's an average of 3 videos per week. You can increase to 4 videos per week, 6 videos per month or even 12 videos per month if you have many clients or potential clients.

    - Results. Once you create the videos, you could have them out in the virtual world and your targeted audience will be receiving your message every time they turn on their computers and choose to engage. Monetizing your channel could bring a steady income stream that you can further promote to grow your income

Video marketing is easy to do and once you get the hang of it, you may be amazed at how many people you may be able to get to watch your videos.

The internet has been evolving in size and shape over the past few years, and what has become a necessity for video is now taking on a life of its own. The latest trend to catch fire is one that lets people do pretty much whatever they want, whenever they want. The craze is really the ability to move around the internet as if you were teleporting, and this is an opportunity that video has no intention of ignoring.

In fact, video has always been all about getting your audience to feel as if they are with you wherever you are.

It's no secret that video is not just here to stay, but that it can become a permanent fixture of the internet. The question is, how can you benefit now from this new era in the way you get your message across?

Here are 3 ways in which video can benefit your business today:

1. Enhanced SEO

A video is generally recognized by search engines more often than text, and this means you can drive more traffic to your site.

With a video, you can use annotations to direct your audience to where you want them to be. With annotations, you are able to include keywords, which makes the video appear in search results.

2. Increased Product Sales

With video, you can demonstrate your products to your audience more times than you ever could with just words. This allows you to connect with your audience on a more personal level. In fact, a video can improve your conversion rate because people feel like they are learning more about your products than they would with text alone.

3. Increased Social Networking

In this day and age, people like to watch videos. Now, you can get thousands of additional views through video. This means more traffic, more subscribers and more links to promote.

43. Search Engine Optimization - New and Relevant Traffic!

SEO stands for Search Engine Optimization and is the process of making websites visible in the search engines. Google is the main search engine, Bing is one of the leading search engines, too. The search engines are the place where you search for information on any topic.

The first step is for you to start making your website visible on the search engines and the best means of doing this is to make your website optimized. This optimization is the process of optimizing your website so that it is search engine friendly and easy to find.

With SEO there are some tools that you have to use. When working on SEO, it is important to use tools that have relevance and are helpful in the process. So it is always a benefit to make use of something like the page rank tool. This tool can inform you of the relevance of your site, the rank that it has among other sites and also the search engine that has a page for your site.

Other tools that are great when working on SEO are the keywords tool and the links tool. When it comes to keywords and links, the keywords tool can allow you to see which keywords you need to use and also the location of other sites that use those keywords.

Link tool can show you which sites are linking to your website and this tool is helpful in the SEO process. You can also see which sites are linking to other sites. In this way, you may be able to have an idea about the competitors of your site.

These tools, like the first tool mentioned above, can help you to make your website more SEO friendly and easy to find on the search engines. SEO is the process of making your website visible in the search engines so that it gets more visitors and also is indexed.

When deciding what marketing strategy to use, the main concern for most businesses is to make money. This is not an easy task. It requires a lot of hard work, management, skill, and creativity. However, this does not have to be expensive. Using the latest technology, marketing strategies are available that can turn your marketing dollars to profits.

Search Engine Optimization (SEO) is one of the latest marketing strategies available. With the help of this marketing technique, you can get massive amounts of exposure and clicks on your website. This makes your website known to a much larger audience. The technology being used is extremely powerful. This makes it easier for you to provide results. This makes your company more visible. As a result, you can generate more traffic and consequently generate more sales.

Keywords

One of the key components of this marketing strategy is keywords. What you have to realize about popular keywords is that they are the most targeted. Use a keyword analytic tool to make sure you find the keywords that have the most searches compared to the level of difficulty to rank high. Once you choose your keywords, the search engine then targets them. This makes it so your website could appear in search results about the keyword. This also makes it easier for the search engine to match your website against the keywords that are being searched. If you have used SEO before, you know that this does mean your content has to be more specific. This also means that you have to make sure that your keywords are very specific. You have to use the right amount of keywords to provide relevant content that is being viewed. Usually, don't use more than five of the same keywords in a blog of 1,000 words.

Here's our guideline for implementing keywords:

-Primary keyword in Title, in the beginning is better.
-Other secondary keyword in the title is good too but only if natural fit
-Primary keyword in the first paragraph, better in the first sentence or beginning of the first paragraph.
-Keywords in H2 tags, especially primary keyword (secondary/section titles)
-Keywords sprinkled naturally in articles (primary keyword preferably 5+ times in an article of 500-1,000 words).

The truth is that a search engine optimization campaign might require a lot of creative skills and technical know-how. There are some ways that you can leverage the expertise of a SEO firm. You can choose a firm that has some experience in this marketing technique. You can ask for an overview of the campaigns they have handled and what is involved. Before signing up with anyone, make sure that you have a written contract with the firm. This is a good way to reduce disputes. For this reason, you should get a written guarantee of your satisfaction.

Getting traffic to your website is the primary goal of every internet entrepreneur. As a matter of fact, the entire idea of building a website or even a blog is to get visitors to your site. More traffic means more sales and more sales means more money.

There are tons of ways to get visitors to your website but the most effective and most affordable SEO methods are SEO link building. Link building is probably the most popular method of getting your site indexed by search engines such as Google.

If you are running a business and you don't have time to search engine optimization, then you can hire someone to do it for you. For those of you who are small business owners and don't have enough time to do SEO, there are affordable and effective SEO methods which you can utilize for free.

1. Blogging is one of the most effective methods of attracting traffic to your site. For this you need to have a blog hosted on the internet. Here you can create posts which can

include keywords such as SEO which might lead traffic to your site. You can create a blog and keep it updated on a regular basis. It is best if you can post your links on the first post of the blog. The links should be inserted at the bottom part of the blog.

2. Social bookmarking is another method of attracting traffic to your site. Here you can post links which might direct traffic to your site. The links should be inserted at the bottom part of the blog.

3. Directory submission is another very effective and affordable SEO method. Here you can submit your site in directories which might direct traffic to your site. It is best if you can submit your website in high trafficked directories. You can also submit your site to the low trafficked directories. This submission is free of cost.

Getting traffic to your website can be difficult especially if you're a small business. You'll find that the best methods for getting traffic have proven to be the methods that aren't expensive, require minimal effort, and are easy to implement. On Page Optimization is one of the most effective methods of getting your website seen by people.

The on page optimization process includes the editing of the content and structure of the website. You'll notice that your website has been optimised into a more attractive website. There are things that you can do that are visible but some are hidden from you. You can use this to your advantage and become noticed by the search engines by doing the hidden SEO techniques.

The hidden SEO technique can help you get your website seen by search engines. This can lead to traffic to your website.

Hidden SEO Techniques:

1. Hidden text can be used to your advantage by editing the HTML code on the website. These codes can be found in the header and footer of your website. Hidden HTML codes can be edited to say something other than what they are.

2. You can create an eCommerce store with your website by using JavaScript with your WordPress blog. This could help to get your store noticed by search engines.

3. You can take the keywords and phrases from the content and paste into your website without attracting search engines.

4. A SEO tactic which is difficult to detect is the creation of doorway pages. This technique can get your website indexed but the search engines can't determine the content of the pages.

The hidden SEO technique is not as effective as on page optimization but it can still help you get your website seen by search engines. You might need to use some of these methods to get your website noticed.

44. Control Quality - Stop Trying to Get Instant Results in Your Marketing

One of the biggest problems I see in business today is that people want instant gratification. They get into a rush and in that rush, many of them buy things they don't need. Many of them trade quality for quantity. The result: They become unhappy and some even have problems, including burnout. This is why I propose that we stop trying to provide instant gratification and start giving people quality in a timely manner.

When you start giving people quality in a timely manner, they should begin to expect it and in turn, become loyal to you and to your quality. This is why I propose that we change our marketing focus from instant gratification to quality in a timely manner.

Today, when we buy things for our businesses, we usually buy based on whether we feel we need it or not. We buy based on whether or not we feel like we need it and based on our bond with a certain feeling of quality. Does that sound familiar? You've bought something before, you've liked it, and now you know exactly what kind of feeling of quality it produced so you want to buy it again and again.

When we start giving our customers quality in a timely and consistent manner, we give them a refresher course in value and what value really means.

We teach them that a lot of money can be wasted on a vanity project or an unnecessary expense that adds nothing to our business, but can add millions to the bottom line of a company that doesn't know what value really is but wants to exploit our unawareness of true value. This is why we should be careful about piling on costs until we are sure they translate directly into value for our customers and our business.

The bottom line is that in order to get quality, we must give them quality, we must have the right tools and culture that is quality-driven. We teach them that in order to get quality, we must provide them quality in a streamlined manner. We then begin to teach them that we must demand quality and by doing so, we begin to control quality.

In the end, we teach them that if we don't give them quality, they won't get quality and in turn, they won't be addicted to our product. So, we begin to control quality.

This is why I propose that we stop trying to provide instant gratification in our marketing and start providing quality products and services in a timely and controlled manner. Remember, the timely aspect is important because the expectation of quality of the customer demands to receive quality. The goal becomes not to simply get a customer, but to keep them loyal and bonded with the quality we give.

With quality comes loyalty and in turn, with loyalty comes value and in turn, with value, comes acceptance/anticipation and in turn, comes success.

If we give them quality, they could reciprocate by doing business with us and in turn, we begin to control the quality in our business and the trajectory of our business.

The key to whether we control the quality in our business or not, is whether or not we control our marketing as a vehicle of quality.

45. Marketing Strategies: A Way of Being Advertised

One of the most common ways that we promote any business is by way of advertising. Advertising isn't limited to newspapers, radio and television, although those are the main ones that most of us are familiar with. Advertising can also be applied on the internet, where companies like Google are formed. It exists in order to give users the best quality results by way of which they can find whatever they are looking for, whenever they are looking for it.

For any business, advertising is vital. It helps in attracting potential clients and customers and also in defining what kind of business you are in. In essence, advertising is a vital aspect of any business in order to gain potential clients and customers. Although, if done incorrectly, it can actually harm your business in a way that can ruin your entire business. This is because if you don't attract the right kind of clients, your business could implode and you won't be able to continue.

As with any business, you may need a way to attract the attention of potential customers and clients. This is important because not only is it beneficial in having potential customers, but also ingraining an image of your company that makes it trustworthy and believable.

This is because any form of advertising can cause your business to go through ups and downs. This is because when you advertise, your potential clients and customers may be attracted to you. This is because advertising is a way of promoting yourself and your products and services. This is also because when they are attracted to you, it means that you are doing your job well.

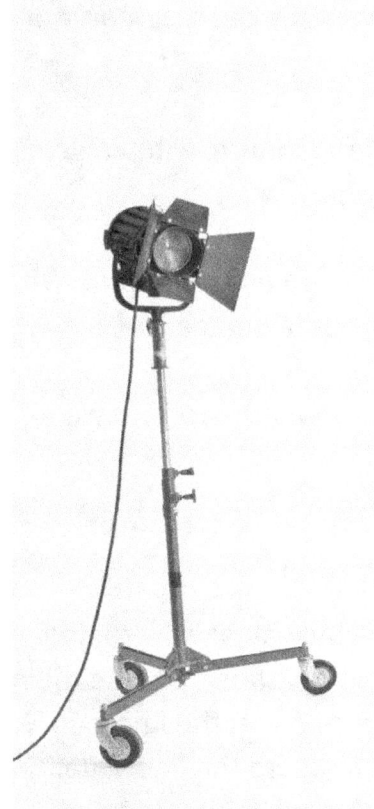
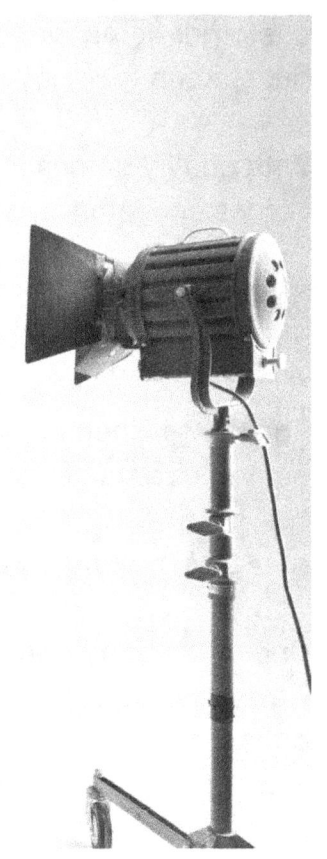

Another thing that you should consider when advertising is the image that you want to give to your business. This can be important because this is a way of defining how you want your business to be known in the end. The most common way of doing this is by how you advertise yourself. For example, if you want your business to be popular, you could need to promote it in a way that focuses on that aspect. If you want your business to be known as a reliable business, you may need to advertise yourself correspondingly. In essence, advertising is a way of promoting your business in a way that fosters sustained growth.

Another important thing to consider when advertising is the type of products that you want to promote. You would need to decide what kind of products to put in order to attract potential customers. For example, if you want to attract potential clients and customers, you may need to promote goods that are practical. This means that when you advertise yourself in a practical way, you should get potential customers attracted to you. When people are attracted to you, they are more likely to purchase your goods. This way, you can earn profits.

What can you do with the profits? You can either spend them on advertising again, or invest them in your business. The former is typically a good way of spending the profits because it also often helps to promote future business and company culture. However, if you want to give a part of the profits away in a meaningful way or create incentives, this is a very good way of giving gifts to your employees and as well as your potential customers and clients in rewards, savings, and limited-time offers. A way of rewarding them for their efforts and incentivizing new business. Of course, you could also invest in other aspects of your business such as operations, capital infrastructure, training, consulting, and so on.

In the end, you have a way of advertising yourself when you employ marketing techniques such as the one that you employ in the article. Of course, you would need to use your own judgement and experience unless you can outsource the entire process. This is because the purpose of this article is to teach you marketing techniques. That is, how to promote your brand in the right image.

The same thing goes for hiring marketing professionals to do the marketing for you. Of course, the latter is usually a very good way of advertising yourself. However, it is not a way of promoting yourself that you can rely on when it comes to the profits forever. You have to be careful in selecting your marketing experts. You need to select a marketing expert that knows how to earn you profits and understands your clientele. That is, a marketing expert that would likely help you to promote your goods by associating with an image that is understandable and trusted by your customers.

46. Affiliate Marketing - How to Build Your List Using Social Media

Affiliate marketing is a fast growing business on the internet. I like the fact that you can be up and running in minutes not days with affiliate marketing. You can set yourself up with little investment and have a growing business within a week's time with no cost taking of cash.

An affiliate marketer is one who markets other people's products and services in exchange for a commission each time one of the purchased items is bought through his own marketing efforts. For example

John was online last week buying a laptop for his daughter. He saw an advert about a 'little toy' that was being 'rediscovered' and purchased the ebook 'how to rediscover the little toy.

Elliot was online a couple of weeks ago and saw a video about a 'little toy' and also purchased the ebook.

Once the items are bought John and Elliot are unaware that an affiliate marketing campaign has been run by the little toy publisher, this may not seem very effective but bear in mind that his purchase was a result of Elliott's own marketing effort and therefore not as lucrative as John's.

If you have not looked into this matter I encourage you to do so as there are hundreds of merchants who can pay you as long as you bring the item to their website and one of your ads on their website, as an affiliate marketer you have to take advantage of this.

As an affiliate marketer you are in the position of promoting the items you come across whilst browsing the web. You are not limited to what you can promote, you can simply spread the information about those products, so that it circulates throughout the world wide web. These products and services are those which many search engines have included in their list of bestsellers.

- Products that have been recommended by many other members and which have a high gravity, high ratings, and high reputation are a good place to start, i.e. bestsellers in the ClickBank market are listed as 'life insurance' or 'diet pills'.

A good affiliate marketing strategy is to promote something which has a low exposure but has been recommended by many members. There is a good chance that the product might be recommended by many other members as well and is therefore likely to circulate throughout the web with a lot of members promoting it.

- You should find items which are highly recommended by many members and promote those items on your site.

To achieve this aim you may ideally wish to build an 'affiliate team' of 'affiliates' and provide them with the 'affiliate tools' so that they are able to promote the items on your site. Another great way to promote affiliate links is to send them out to email lists of people who have subscribed through a landing page. You can use various services that merge email marketing, landing pages, and affiliate marketing capabilities into a single streamlined platform similar to Convertkit or others.

If you're the vendor, you can also build an 'affiliate team' by creating an 'affiliate directory' which lists all the products and services on your site.

- Another way of promoting items on your site is by creating a 'social media site' which is not an affiliate program, but provides members with the ability to promote items which are available on your site. Such sites are often linked to affiliate directories and 'affiliates' can then use the site to promote the item they are promoting.

One great feature of such sites is that you can build a large list of subscribers and use these lists to promote items which you promote on your site. This can enable you to market the items you promote far more effectively and quickly.

Here is a simple example to help you to see how this works. Say you have built a big list of subscribers using email marketing and you have 1,000 opt-in subscribers to your email list. Then you can promote an item and offer them a free sample of the item such as a video or audio file (as a thank you for leaving your email address).

I can give you an example of how this can work. You have a website with 500 opt-ins and you send a promotional email to this list. So now you have 1,000 opt-in subscribers from before and 500 people get the email (who visited your website). So they are now going to see your promotional email and might be more likely to take action if they have the free sample item.

This technique can work for any size of list, of course. However, the point is this: What if instead of sending an email to 500 people, you would send an email to 500,000 people?

That is more people and therefore more people can receive your promotion. Of course, the other thing to consider is to make sure that the promotion should be good and not junk, because junk may result in the email being marked as spam and the promotion not getting seen.

This is an example of how this 'social media' concept works and could help you to build the most popular list possible. As you see, you can combine social media marketing, email marketing, affiliate marketing, and video marketing to promote your product in a multi-dimensional way. Typically, the more tools you merge and master, the greater the likelihood of success.

Note: Although these examples show how you can use social media to build a big list, the concept is general and can be applied to different websites. It just has to be part of your strategy to think of different types of list building.

47. Affiliate Marketing - 3 Ways to Be Successful

This article looks at the two main reasons people join affiliate marketing programs and then proceed to fail at them. The reasons are simple, many people don't like the idea of setting up their own business and getting involved with the day to day aspects of running an offline business. Also many people are not used to dealing with the stress and pressure of running an online business. Finally many people don't see the need to put in the effort and time required to succeed.

It is important to note that this article looks at the day to day work of an affiliate marketer. It does not look at the skills required to succeed or at the resources required to achieve success. This segment could also look at the skill of creating a profit from affiliate marketing programs. The skills are the ability to generate targeted traffic and the ability to sell a suitable product.

The day to day work of an affiliate marketer is a pretty monotonous process. It requires a certain amount of self discipline and the desire to succeed. After that the prospect of setting up an online business is not as difficult as most people think it is. There are a lot of free means available to achieve success, this article is not meant to knock them nor is it intended to discredit them. This part is merely looking at the reasons most people fail and what can be done to succeed.

The two main reasons most people fail are lack of self motivation and the lack of relevant skills required to succeed.

Self-motivation is a complicated issue. Most people think they can be inspired by watching a sales letter or reading a testimonial, but it is more often the result of lack of effort. If you don't have the desire to work on your business then it can be difficult to motivate yourself to carry out the tasks required to succeed.

Lack of passion: most people think they could be able to copy someone else and get the same level of results, but it is not always the case. The true test of your ability to get results is the effort you put in. Most people are willing to copy someone else if the person they copied has strong results. The same applies to affiliate programs. The stronger your desire is to succeed the more work you may have to put in to get similar results.

On the other hand you need relevant skills, otherwise you could be overconfident for a bad reason and this could cause you to overestimate your actual results and hence decrease your efficiency. A dose of reality is always helpful to get you back on track. Never forget the end goal, though. You will likely face many droughts before you find the oasis of affiliate marketing. The only way to overcome this problem is to learn a new skill or discover a new resource every day, which is not a simple task.

So having a solid desire to succeed is more important than having relevant skills. But these reasons are not the only reasons most people fail in their affiliate marketing attempts.

So if you want to succeed, this is what you must do to get that goal you want:

1. Develop a new skill: Do not be fooled by the fact that you don't have a skill right now. In order to get that goal you want, you need a new skill. Develop a new skill so that you can tackle challenging tasks and achieve results. In addition, find new resources and ways to help your cause. Don't be afraid to jump ship either if you see something doesn't work out as planned. This could happen many times until you start to make progress.

2. Develop a plan: You must have a plan of action so that you are on the right track. If you don't have a plan you can just go through life getting the spur of the moment decisions. But if you have a plan, then you may be able to understand your decisions and take the correct action accordingly.

3. Put things in order: Before you take any action, ask yourself whether your plan of action is in order. If your plan of action is not in order, then you may not be able to take the required action.

Once you have done these 3 things, your desire can increase so that you may be able to put in order the skills you have so that you can go through life without fear of failure. If you do one thing each day, and you are willing to do more, you might be able to achieve goals in life more easily.

48. Tips to Improve Your Website

We've all probably been there. You've done your homework, you've targeted your site correctly, and you've done your research. So far so good. But after clicking on a link you land on a page that just burns a hole in your pocket and makes you sick. What do you do? You click again and again but the page doesn't change and you still get sicker. It's like clicking on the same page over and over again. It's like going to a room that smells like mothballs, the walls and ceiling look like they've been sprayed with Bondo, and the furniture is like an undertaker's chamber.

There's no denying it, if you visit a web site and it smells bad, or looks outdated, or has a gross scent that no amount of washing or wax should get rid of, you're going to click away as fast as your legs can carry you. If your web page has a gross odor, or even just a smelly background, you're going to wonder why you ever got involved with the web in the first place. Now, I'm speaking figuratively, but I think you get the point. Nobody really wants to associate with an outdated or incoherently-designed website because it shows the creator is not dedicated to their craft.

You're going to wonder how anyone thought they could get away with putting that stink in the first place.

This is the dilemma web designers and marketers face every single day. And so, many web designers have simply moved on to the next thing when they come across pages that just don't work. Or that they are plain and ugly. Or just plain wrong.

But when you come across pages that work, the feeling you get from visiting them is... Oh my gosh, they're working!

They are beautiful, and they are just what you want them to be. You are full of energy and hope, and you feel like you're finally going to get what you've been looking for all these years. You likely want to give them all your money, and you want to become a part of the web design community. So what are you supposed to do?

There is one thing you can do. Buy your dream web design, and design it right!

So you have one single thing to go on, and that is the website you are going to design. And as you visit the various web design sites, you are going to see lots of buzzwords, and you're going to be asking yourself... Is this web design for me? Is what I'm seeing right for me?

What you're going to find out is that most of these sites are not the right fit for you, simply because they are not designed right for you. And so what you're going to do is go to the sites that have the right fit, and right for you. But you're going to have to put in a little work.

Wherever you do your work, you are going to need a lot of imagination. You're going to need a lot of creativity. But more than that, you're going to need a lot of dedication, and some serious patience.

But most of all, you're going to need to love what you're doing. You're going to need to love what you're seeing. And when you come across a design site that's love, you can know you've found the right web design company for you. And this is what we mean by the right web design community.

A website is a collection of information about a company. Information on the website is generally provided by a third party or written material and it is designed to inform, educate, connect, promote, generate leads, engage, sell, build your brand and connect with your audience. This can be done by providing summaries and overviews of various products and services in your portfolio or by providing comprehensive information about your company. There are different ways to design a website and a designer needs to be virtually aware of them all.

This is basically the construction and upgrading of a website. Content Management Systems or CMS are very popular today and with various online CMS platforms emerging every day, it is a practical tool to utilize content on your website. With the CMS it is very easy to manage your content and add new pages or information. Content can be updated in real time or periodically. This way you can maintain your brand equity with the user base without having to go to the developer every time you want to update something. It also has an advantage of being search engine friendly when set up correctly.

This is the addition of additional pages or information to your original website. This is a great way to grow your company if you have a lot of content already or start with small information and later on grow your website by adding additional pages or information. In this case the designer can employ the CMS or apply search engine techniques to expand your site in various ways. Some SEO techniques also help in this.

Designing a website is a challenging task and at the same time very rewarding as well. A professionally designed website may not only bring you leads but also your company's image may grow with time. You should be able to grow your company's brand equity with time, without going to the developer every time you want to add something.

In addition, you can easily outsource website design to freelancers on sites like Upwork and Fiverr. These offer great alternatives at much more affordable prices if you want an expert doing the design for you.

However, once the website is done and shiny, the real work begins. It's time to make a splash by learning all the different ways of connecting and reaching out to your future customers!!

49. How To Make Emails With Affiliate Products More Effective

In order to be successful in this type of marketing, there are certain strategies that must be employed. These strategies are:

1) Make the Email seem very relevant to the recipient

Make sure the email appears very relevant to the recipient. They do not just want an email about a special offer from the company. They want to know, This is a special offer, and I'm going to do something nice for you.

2) Use a very attractive subject line

The subject line of the email is the key to success of your email marketing campaign. This should contain something that can trigger an action such as special offers, discount, reward, money back guarantee etc.

3) Use a catchy but beneficial subject line

If the recipient is tickled by the subject line, they are then more inclined to open the email. A well-designed subject line may entice the recipient into opening the email. The subject line must contain a bit of personality and a little drama, or else the email is most likely going to be deleted.

By making sure that the email is short, and the recipient is interested in what you are offering them, you give yourself a chance. With this strategy, you are able to get the recipient hooked. You are sending information out to them. What you are going to be doing with the emails is you are going to be tracking, on a minute basis, how many people opened the email and how many people clicked through to your website. You are going to be tracking that in order to improve your marketing strategies. The idea here is that if you can get a click through rate of 3%, it means that three out of every 100 people who opened the email clicked on your link to your website.

These are just some ideas about how the use of email marketing can improve your business. It is a powerful and a smart way to boost your sales when done right. You can link it with affiliate links. The use of email marketing is something that you need to do to get to that next level. The idea of the use of email marketing is to remind your recipients to buy what you are selling. This idea is still going strong because all companies are working on it to find new ways to convince the customers to buy what they are selling.

By using e-newsletters, you are able to keep in touch with your customers and gain trust from them. E-newsletters can be your email that you send to your customers. The idea of this business is to enhance your relationship with your customers and gain trust from them.

It is easier to sell to people who already know who you are and where you're from. It may not be hard to get email addresses from your customers but it is going to be difficult to get email addresses from potential customers. The idea here is to make your email address list a list of people who are already interested in what you're selling. In doing so, you can generate sales from your business.

The idea here is to build a good and a responsive email list. This business is designed to get new subscribers and to keep the ones that you already have. This business works on your existing list to sell your products and services. It is also very useful to have a list of emails of your customers.

The idea of building a good and a responsive email list of your customers is to make your email addresses list a list of the people who are already interested in what you're selling. In doing so, you can generate sales from your business.

Email newsletters give you the capability to send emails to many people at the same time. It is also a great idea to use an autoresponder that you can find on the internet as a way to help you gain subscribers.

If you use email providers like Gmail, consider downloading some plugins that have many fancy templates you can integrate right into your email. Adding some colors could be helpful, but avoid flaunting too much. Add a call-to-action towards the end of the email (and sometimes in the beginning) with a button or sign-up form. Make it easy for your customers to click on your links and buttons without appearing too salesy or pushy. Most-importantly, stay consistent with your marketing design and layout.

50. What You Should Know About Blogging and How to Use It

The content on your blog is crucial to your blog's success. This article explains the importance of your blog content and how to write posts that people want to read.

What makes a blog successful, for the most part, is the content. Yes, you can have great content that's fun to read, but if nobody is reading it, then you won't be able to do any sales or earn any money from it. So you need SEO.

Writing content is sometimes the easy part. Getting people to read it is the hard part.

If you have good content, then you don't need to worry about people reading it once they do. You can just relax and enjoy the ride. Either way, you should feel at ease with the topic or niche you select. It should be something you know plenty about.

Content Marketing Part 1: Find Your Niche

The first thing that you need to do is to find out what your niche is. Your niche is basically the thing that you're going to talk about in your blog. It could be virtually anything from home improvement to computer programming to dog grooming. Just think about what you're passionate about and can talk about without thinking too much.

Once you've decided on what your niche is, you need to do some research. Find out what others are talking about in your niche. Research the competition. There are different ways of doing this. One of the best ways is to visit forums that are in your niche. This is the best way to find out how strong your competition is. You can also use Google search, and look at the site's page. Look at their Top sites and their Page Rank. Just make sure that you do some research before you post something on your blog.

Content Marketing Part 2: Create Content that People Want to Read

Once you have decided on your niche, then it's time to create some content. You have to remember that the most important part of writing content is to write content that people want to read. It's not about creating something that could impress the reader. You have to make the reader enjoy what you wrote. This comes from the fact that the best selling books have the readers who love the book because it's written by a fellow writer. The reader enjoys what the writer is writing because this writer is a good writer. The reader may also enjoy the ending because the writer has brought the story to its conclusion. All of this makes the reader say "Okay, this writer is good, I'll check out his blog".

These are the only things that you need to do when you start out in the Blogging world. There are many more things that you can do. These are just the basics. One of the best ways to post your ideas is to post a blog post and if you have any great ideas, then you can do a webinar with your blog. Whatever you do, remember that you have to be patient and keep taking actions. You can reap the benefits soon enough if the wind goes in your favor

51. Is Your Blog Operating On All Foundations?

This segment will focus on how to blog in order to produce fantastic and viral content that leads to traffic generation and profitability in affiliate marketing. If you are an affiliate marketer, you probably realize that marketing products and programs is essential to your business and ultimately the success of your business. But, in order to succeed, you need the right strategies. A blog is a great way to generate organic traffic to your site from keywords that people type into search engines. The higher your blog ranks in search engines, the easier it should be to find and the easier you can attract new customers to your affiliate business.

Here are some key factors to consider when starting your blog:

1. How to prime customers with your blog to make lots of purchases? You are the content provider or creator, which means you post the content that is written or provided by you, as an affiliate, to your particular product or program.

2. How to use your blog to cater to the right segment of traffic or visitors that your particular product or program requires? How to blog the keyword or keywords that your particular product or program generates and how to blog that traffic to your particular program, product, or service in order to complete a sale?

3. How to collect the contact information of your visitors in order to add them to your mailing list or newsletter for future sales?

4. How to create a blog that can go viral or can be shared in shorter formats on other platforms like social media? Also, how to recycle the same information to create various types of mediums like written blogs, podcasts, videos, and so on.

5. How to blog to convince your readers that you are a trustworthy source and how to convince your readers that your product is the best match for them. In order to do so, don't just assume that they are ready to buy. It's better to convince your future customers why they should get behind your product or service with some clear benefits and comparisons with competitors. This doesn't have to be a complicated thing. Simply state the area where you are better and explain why in simple language. Focus on the benefit the customer receives. Discover what emotion is driving customers to buy your product and cater to that particular emotion.

If you do not blog your traffic, no one else could do it for you. Your best move is to blog your traffic using lots of exciting content. If you're not excited about writing or creating it, then your audience likely won't be enticed by it either. Great content feels exciting to create and relive again and again. Keep improving your content. The traffic that comes to your site is the traffic that you create as a result of your inspired blogging. If you have not built up traffic for your program or product, no one else can.

There are many ways to blog, the first of which is to use your own blog, which is better than a self-hosted blog for affiliate marketing purposes, is to use a free platform like WordPress or Blogger. You can also choose to self-host your own blog. I will explain both of these options, but first of all, what is a blog? A blog is a type of informative website that was first introduced to the Internet in 1997 I believe.

A blog is a part of a public-access website which is accessible to the public with little to no restriction. This means that virtually anyone who can access the internet can read your blog and everyone who visits your blog can leave a comment in your blog.

When people visit your blog, they can leave comments. Each time that a person leaves a comment, that person is allowed to put a link to their website in the comment. In most cases, the website that is being referenced must have an adsense (Google AdSense) program, or else the comment will probably be rejected. Networks of blogs with links are likely to rank better and produce a larger social "splash." The links going from one blog to another are called external links. The links connecting different blog posts within the same blog or website are called "internal links."Both internal and external links are used by search engines to measure the structure and eventually rank your blog or website. Hence, the link structure is quite important in SEO.

When you are creating your blog, you should consider how long the blog post should be in terms of word count. Short blogs range anywhere from 300 to 1,000 words, and longer blogs can even surpass 10,000 blogs. The average top-ranking blog seems to be around 1,500 words, but that doesn't mean that a shorter blog can't rank high. The main thing is to focus on great content that your readers will probably want to come back for more.

52. How to Make Your Blog's Content Fresh and Relevant

Blogging is fast becoming one of the most popular topics for online business in this day and age. The blogging trend is continuing to grow stronger and more popular year after year. Blogging isn't simply about just making an online journal. The best bloggers have more of a desire to communicate with their readers. A truly popular blog can eventually become a trusted resource by your readers.

It's the readers that you're communicating with that makes a blog a best-liked blog. In fact, a blog that's received much attention can ultimately become an online business that's more valuable to the reader. Here are some tips on becoming a best-liked blog in just a few short years.

1. Write quality content

The best-liked blogs will probably always be those that provide quality content for their readers. It's important to make sure that you offer what your readers want. Without this quality, you'll simply become a business that's more popular for its points than for the content itself. Don't disappoint your readers.

2. Don't just write about what you "heard"

People can tell you all day about what you heard about. It's important to remember that people buy based on what they hear, not what they read. This means that the best-liked blogs will probably always be those that provide information that your readers can act upon.

3. Put value in what you write about

You're likely to be successful in your blog if you always put value into what you're writing about. The best-liked blogs are often those that provide great content and products that your readers can act upon. This means that the blog should be about the topic that you're writing about. This way, your blog can eventually be seen as a place that people can act upon and can act upon fast. The speed is important because once a visitor acts upon your blog, they'll want more from your blog.

4. Make your blog's content fresh and relevant

When a visitor finds your blog, what they want is fresh, relevant information. If you have to refresh the content on your blog, make sure you always provide it in a topical manner. This is what your readers want. If they want fresh, relevant information, they'll sign up to your RSS feed, subscribe to your email, or check your blog's statistics. The best way to get the fresh, relevant content that your visitors want is to have an RSS feed that provides the information that they're looking for.

5. Instead of recycling information from other blog posts, download books in pdf!

There are several sites like Pdf Drive that allow you to download thousands of books for free. Simply download the book in a pdf file and use it as a source of information for your blog. Obviously, you can't just copy-paste from the book, but you can use it to paraphrase and take information from it. In case you need academic sources, most books already provide them. In addition, you can use the control-F button to search for specific keywords inside the book to save you time. Using a book can make your blogs stand out with rich content that isn't simply recycled from other top-ranking articles, which can result in poorer rankings for you.

What is WordPress.org?

WordPress is an Open Source application. The source code is available on its website. The application is developed by volunteers. There are thousands of plugins available, maybe more. WordPress is also available as a set of plugins. It is the "father" of blogging platforms some would argue.

You can manage almost all aspects of your website through the use of WordPress. You can make amendments to the website or you can also upgrade your WordPress application to the most recent version. There are a huge number of applications which are WordPress based. This opens up options for the users who are not happy with the software which they have. You can also keep your application working on the latest version.

A WordPress application has the ability to manage the themes. It also has the ability to install plug-ins. This enables you to add many functions to your website. It also has the ability to send email and to manage comments. This enables you to manage and manage your users well. You can add categories. This helps to keep your content organized and on topic. WordPress also has the ability to create images, which are hyperlinks, and it also has the ability to publish your content on the web.

WordPress has the ability to link your WordPress content to your website. This is important as it allows search engines to index your website. It also has the ability to install widgets which allow you to create an opt-in list or even a no-cost newsletter list. This helps you to create a following. It also has the ability to create RSS feeds. This is important to allow your users to subscribe to your content. It also has the ability to set up a mailing list. This enables you to communicate with your subscribers.

And this is just a small corner of the benefits of using WordPress to run your website. It has many other benefits, which we will not discuss here. However, WordPress is a little more difficult to master. Other newer providers like GoDaddy or Wix make it easy for you to design your website on the fly, but they are modern adaptations of the functions that WordPress has traditionally performed. It's hard to say which one is better. It all depends on your needs. Do some thorough research before choosing your provider as this decision could be hard to reverse once it's made.

53. Advertise Your Business With a Story

The first step in advertising your business is to create a story. A story is the backbone of an advertisement, but it is the details of your story that determine its success or failure. There are three basic elements to a story: the Protagonist, the Obstacle, and the Resolution.

The Protagonist - this person is the hero of the story, and is the central focus of the advertisement.

The Obstacle - this is the challenge the Protagonist faces.

The Resolution - this is the resolution of the challenge or the accomplishment of the Protagonist.

We call the Protagonist the Event or the Spark of the Story. All events begin with the Protagonist. Once the Protagonist is established, all other events in the story must be driven by and center on the Protagonist. This is known as the Protagonistic Modeling of Events.

The story may have numerous Resolution(s) but the Protagonist is the one that drives the Event or Spark of the Story. It is the Protagonist who causes all of the events in the story to happen in the way that they do.

Because the Protagonist is the driving force of the story it is essential to define the Protagonist in advance. You must know who you could be advertising to and how they respond to your products. This can determine the products you can create and other elements of the design of your advertising campaign. The Protagonist can be a person, place, thing or idea.

To select the Protagonist requires a level of planning and analysis that goes beyond merely writing an advertising slogan and running an ad campaign. The Protagonist is defined by the combination of all of the things that are true about the Subject and all of the things that are not true about the Subject. This should allow you to pinpoint the Protagonist and direct the events in the story to produce an advertising campaign that produces results.

The characters, or the personalities of the characters are what make up the main characters of the campaign. You must create as many different characters as you can, but they can't be the Protagonist. This is the only one character who can't be changed, turned around, or overcome in some way. In fact they cannot be defeated. Let's say you are selling a brand of lotion or skin cream. An example of such a main character is someone who struggles from perpetual dry and peeling skin, especially after they move to Colorado where it is really dry.

The Protagonist faces problems but in the end must triumph over every obstacle and overcome them in the way that he does. This is accomplished with the help of the product or service that you are selling. In other words, the story presents a value proposition of whatever you're selling to your audience.

54. Busy, Busy, Busy - Stop!

I had a client who was running a business out of her basement. This isn't unheard of, but there are a couple of reasons she chose to do this. One was to make herself more efficient as she was running more than one business simultaneously. The other reason was to create a sense of community in her home. To make it a mini village bustling with activity.

We live in an era where many of us have more choices in our daily lives than our parents did. Our work demands us to make choices about work and family life, but more than that, we have choices about what community, be it virtual, we want to live in. This makes our lives a whirlwind of activity and activity has come to replace a calm mind with furious chattering of the mind. And while thoughts help us zoom in or focus on a particular detail, it's easy to lose sight of the big picture.

One of the ways busyness undermines our progress is when we give in to our busyness. This has a tendency to undermine our ability to focus on the big scheme of things. It puts an emphasis on the urgency of things. It's easy to be seduced by this and get ourselves "all caught up" in the trap of business.

Drucker describes busyness as "excessively difficult and hurried activity."

Focusing is the antidote to this. It's defined as "the art of speeding up by slowing down."

To put it another way, it's the art of stopping the redundant activities and introducing innovation and new ways to do things.. It's described as a choice between two courses of action. One is the easy one and the other is the difficult one. This is where we use the Stoic principle of the right choice. The Stoics see it as avoiding the painful and not doing the impossible.

So, If you feel like you're getting bogged down mentally, it's time to stop and energize. Try laying on your back and feeling your body from within. Meditation is the art of taking your mind off thinking into pure observation of "what is." If you're constantly thinking about your business, you can lose sight of new possibilities for your business that you haven't yet considered. That's why it's so important to periodically take a step back and look at the big picture. Analyze your strategy. Draw it as a diagram on a piece of paper. Research new ways to promote your business, to improve how it functions. Solutions are already out there -- it's a question of having mental space for them.

55. Top Time Management Tips - Don't be a Slave to Your Phone

Time Management Tips:

There are lots of tips for time management; however we'll share here some for the everyday management of your time.

- Do the important things first: The first task on every day should be to make sure that your important tasks are completed the day before. This is very important because it starts your day off right.

- Do the easy things first: Next time you have a busy schedule try to make sure that you do the easy things first. This means make sure your work is out of the way on your to-do list. Don't work on your business and personal projects while on hold with customer service.

- Do what you have to do: If you have something important to do and it is critical to your job then do it first.

- Eliminate dead time: Most people spend large amounts of time on things that aren't really necessary. This means if you are focused on your work and see fit to keep a busy schedule then watch how you spend your time.

- Don't multitask: There is a fine line between multitasking and multitasking too much. Most people think that they can do 2 things at once. This is a big mistake because it takes a lot of time and energy. We recommend that you do one task at a time for better focus.

- Limit your email checking: Set a limited time frame for checking your email. Most people spend 2-4 hours a day on email. This is often a big mistake because you are wasting time and energy. Also be sure to delete the old emails and only keep the new ones.

- Don't start until you have finished: Start your day by finishing your tasks. This means don't leave things until the last minute. If you have a big task, do something about it before you start.

Time Management Tips - Don't be a slave to your phone.

- When you are on the phone it takes away time from the important tasks on your list. You'll be more productive on the computer, but it's better to be on the phone and complete more tasks quickly, instead of spending an hour on the computer and finishing. Actually, it all depends on the nature of the business, but you get my point. Try to be as efficient with your work time as you can, but without hurrying.

- Don't let your phone take over your life. We recommend that you set specific times where you want to answer your phone. This way it should not interrupt your flow. Instead, answer it when it rings, and move on.

- Don't ask your phone to do the work for you. The phone is not meant to do the work. If you set a specific time to take calls, ask them to call you back within that time. You can get more work done and be more efficient.

- Don't multitask: If you have several important tasks on your list, don't start any of them more than once. All of them can be too overwhelming. Instead, complete each task once and move on.

56. Search Engine Optimization - The Secret to Online Profits

If you are a webmaster, you may be familiar with the concept of PageRank. This is an algorithm for calculating the relevancy of a web page. You may have also heard about other search engines like Google and Bing, but did you know that you can have your web page listed in these search engines through some simple steps?

The first thing you need to understand is that a web page needs to be properly optimized in order for it to appear in Google, Yahoo, and Bing. Now, if you are already familiar with the concept of PageRank and how it works, then you already have a basic understanding on how to get your website listed in these search engines.

You may also have heard about some of the other search engines, but did you know that you can have your web page listed in these search engines through some simple steps? It's easy, and this can even help your search engine optimization efforts because you are in control of your listing, and how your site is listed.

The first thing you need to understand is that a web page needs to be properly optimized in order for it to rank high on Google, Yahoo, and Bing. Exceptions do exist, and sometimes content is truly king. That's why if you had to choose between great content with poor SEO and poor content with good SEO, go for the former.

So what does SEO mean? It means that your site is well designed, and carefully built for the search engines to find it. A sitemap allows for search consoles to find your website. So now you may ask what is meant by well designed. It simply means that your website has many keywords (website content) and these keywords are well positioned in the site's content. The beauty of this is that once it is properly optimized, you may also schedule it to appear in several search engines.

Finding the Right Keywords

If you want your website to be found by the search engines you need to get ranked high on their results. This can be achieved by ranking high on Google page ranks, Yahoo Site Explorer, or Bing, depending on the niche that you are operating in. This article will discuss how to get high page rank on Google, Yahoo, and Bing.

The first thing you need to do is find keywords that best describe your site. You can find keywords by using some of the free keyword suggestion tools available, such as Google AdWords Keyword Tool. You can also search for keywords on Google and look at how many times they are searched for as well as other related searches. Also, take time to read the pages on your site for ideas. Some sites are very popular because they have the keywords in their titles and content and other sites have them because they are popular.

Then you need to find the popularity of the term on the internet. You can find popularity through Web Stats. This allows you to see the number of pages indexed in Google, Yahoo, and Bing. Also, it should give you a site popularity index. This index number is the number on the lower right of the results page. This number can give you the popularity of the site. The higher the number the more popular the site. Of course, you can get the results for the last page to rank on your homepage. You can see this information using the Google Analytics tool.

When you are looking for keywords you also need to consider the competition. You need to choose keywords that have little competition. A low number is usually better because it means you should have a higher click through rate.

Keywords are very important when it comes to SEO. You need to find the most popular and have them on your site. The main keywords that you should be looking for are the terms that your audience is using to find your site. After you have the best keywords for your site, then you need to find ways to use them.

It is important to see the best ways to incorporate the best keywords into your site. This includes the blog posts, images, pages, and articles. You should never forget to use the best keywords when it comes to the search engines.

The Importance of Links to Your Website

Imagine you have a well written article for publication on your site that will likely attract readers. You have included references, as well as keyword phrases that relate to the topic of your article. You are ready to post to your site.

Now you need links to your site. These links should come from well written, quality sites that can also draw readers to your site.

The quality of your site as well as the content of your link is important to the success of your link campaign.

What you want is for other sites to want to link to your website. This can occur when their visitors are satisfied with the content of your site, and that other site is attractive to their visitors.

The links should appear naturally within your content, and should only be created when there is a direct correlation between the two sites.

The visitors of the better sites can link to your site indirectly, because they find your site interesting or helpful.

Here are some examples of how this works. You have a product that is top notch, and you post content about your product on a top notch website. People who use that website may also use the link, and they link to your site because of the content that you post on that site. You have a site with lots of helpful information, and many people use your link to get to your site. Other blogs can post your link directly, because they are also looking for posts that relate to their topic. Finally, other sites that are not quite as helpful may not link at all, because they are not worth the effort.

As you can see, link building does not always have to be a complex procedure. There are several methods that work well, and others that do not. It really comes down to your creativity and the quality of your content.

There is no doubt that if you have a website, you will probably want to attract visitors. If you want to attract them you need to make them aware of your website. This can be done in a number of ways, which include SEO, PPC or CPM (Pay Per Click), however, it is obvious that it is usually better to go for CPM (Cost Per Thousand Impressions) if you're just starting out.

The reason for this is that it can cost you a lesser amount of money. If you perform SEO and PPC then you are probably going to make them think twice about clicking on your site. On the other hand, if you perform CPM then they should only pay for every thousand impressions.

Now you need to decide what method you could use for your site to make them aware of it. Well, it is best if you perform a cost per click as it is more likely to get people to click on your site. For this you would likely need to ensure the keyword/phrase that you may be using is in your URL or header. The best thing about this is that you likely need to ensure that your site is ranked well for your targeted keyword/phrase. This is because the search engines can use this as a factor in determining your ranking. By ensuring that your site is well ranked you are more likely to get people to click on your site.

The key thing to note here is that it takes time to build up your position. It is best that you perform a CPM campaign so that you can reap the benefits more quickly. This is also a good way to avoid wasting your money on the PPC. CPM campaigns are often great because they are cheap and effective. This is the reason why many site owners choose to use them. The fact that it is cost effective also helps to bring many more people to your site. However, not all CPM's are so good. You'll have to experiment to find that special sauce that works for you.

57. Top 5 Blogging Tips

It is important to ensure that your blog content is always high quality. When visitors get to your blog they should feel that it is fresh and appealing and the words you use to promote your business should be appealing for the search engine spiders. One of the best ways to do this is to avoid writing long sentences for your blog posts. It is usually best to use short sentences and use short words. These help to make the blog posts readable and they are also important for the search engine spiders. The following are other ways to ensure that your blog content is always high quality.

1. Use short sentences- Your blog posts should be easy to read and you should try to avoid long sentences because they make your content look boring. This means that you should use short sentences for your blog posts.

2. Use short words and sentences- These are also important for the search engine spiders. They help to make your posts readable and they also help for the search engine spiders to get the most out of reading your posts. These short words are: noun, verb, adjective and other words.

3. Use numbers and letters- You should use numbers and letters for your blog posts. These help for the search engine spiders to get information. The following are the numbers and letters.

A. Cite Referring sources- This helps for the search engine spiders to find other relevant content for their search.

B. Use Keywords- This helps for the search engine spiders to get the most out of your content. When you use keywords, they should be able to quickly see the most relevant content for their search.

C. Include tags and description- This is also an important aspect of the blog posts. You should include tags and a description. A tag is a word that you put next to a post that helps the search engine spiders to easily find the post that they should be checking out.

5. Update your blog-

1. Your posts should be frequent - You should try to post to your blog at least once a day when you're getting started. The reason behind this is that the search engine spiders can be checking out your blog when they crawl your site. When you post to your blog, they will in many cases be able to easily access it and this can help your blog to get more visibility on the web.

2. Write articles - Writing articles on your blog posts can be a great way to update your blog and help the search engine spiders find new content for their search. When you write an article, try to make sure that it is focused and brief.

3. Use social media - You should always keep your blog updated with the latest information on your social media networks. You should do this daily.

4. Submit to directories - This is important to update your blog with the latest information on your blog. When you submit to directories, your website can get found in the search engines. This helps for the search engine spiders to find your site when they are looking for your website.

5. Socialize with your friends and followers - You should always keep your blog updated with the latest information on your social media networks. When you socialize with your friends and followers, it can help the SEO spiders find your posts.

Blogging is a great marketing tool that you should consider using. It is a great way to reach out to the people that you are marketing to and get them involved with your business. It helps you to stay updated with the latest trends and helps to get you noticed on the web. Do remember that blogging should always be done on a regular basis to help the SEO spiders find your website.

Warning: this information is subject to change!

58. Learn These 5 Skills to Become a Real Millionaire Entrepreneur

Have you ever had to learn a new skill? Have you ever had to invest time, money and effort learning a new skill? Well, I bet most of us have spent a good amount of time learning that skill. For that matter, I bet we have invested a good amount of money and time as well. The difference between the newbie and the seasoned pro is that the seasoned pro has honed his or her skill to the point that they can deploy it on a moment's notice.

If that is the case, and you are thinking of getting into business, here is a list of skills you should learn. These skills are not difficult to learn, nor are they difficult to master. They all have an end game.

1. Strategy: Strategy is the science of choosing one's destinations carefully. It is the art of determining which roads are safe and which are not.

2. Marketing: Marketing is the science of making oneself known and connecting with those that need our help. It is the art of building networks that lead to profitable future endeavors.

3. Sales: Sales is the science of buying and selling products and services that align with what the strategy requires. It is the art of closing deals that give the destination one has chosen the outcome one desired.

4. Management: Management is the art of managing oneself and one's business. It is the science of keeping the goals in sight and preventing setbacks. It is the skill of recognizing talent, and utilizing it.

5. Engineering: Engineering is the art of designing things that actually happen. It is the science of convincing people that what one plans actually happens in reality.

Of course, if you are a newbie entrepreneur, you don't have the skill set to make things happen. That's okay. As you go along, you could pick up things along the way. And then you can decide whether you want to use them or not.

1. Networking: Networking is the art of building relationships and convincing people that you are worth their time. It is the science of establishing connections that give one a leg up in the future.

2. Writing: Writing is the science of communicating thoughts and ideas quickly and effectively. It is the art of knowing how to say what is needed without using words.

It has been my experience that most of the people who come to me for business advice don't really know what they want. Often they'll come to me, often with a vision, often just to ask me for a favor. In other words, they don't really know how they're going to make their business happen. I can definitely relate to that. In my life, I've taken on several jobs that were either "just a bridge too far", or just a way to keep me busy, or just something that I enjoyed doing.

But, I've always developed my business with my main goal in mind - to be in business for myself.

I'm in a business because I can. And I've always developed my business around my passions - being home with my family, having fun, helping others, and working for myself. In fact, at the moment, I'm in the exact opposite phase of my business development - I've developed my business around making money.

So I've developed my business around my goals and my passions. My business is not a vehicle for me, it's a vehicle for my clients. I get to be me and help other people be more authentic and authentic helps them to be them.

To answer your specific question, I think that when you're in the phase of your business development where you're working on making money and only making money is always exciting - but is also most-always a challenge. Think about the value you're creating for others, not the money you'll get in return. A service-oriented perspective can help you maintain a high level of customer service.

One final thing - when you're in the phase of your business development where you're working on making money, you have to remember that people are buying what they need to be in touch with their authentic self. And this is always more fun if you are on the same wavelength as your client. So what you're working on has to be what your client is wanting.

Good luck!

www.ingramcontent.com/pod-product-compliance
Lightning Source LLC
Chambersburg PA
CBHW081431220526
45466CB00008B/2341